A Life of Conversion

Meeting Christ in the Gospels

Nihil Obstat
Msgr. Michael Heintz, Ph.D.
Censor Librorum

Imprimatur
✠ Kevin C. Rhoades
Bishop of Fort Wayne-South Bend
July 6, 2019

Except where noted, the Scripture citations used in this work are taken from the *Revised Standard Version of the Bible — Second Catholic Edition* (Ignatius Edition), copyright © 1965, 1966, 2006 National Council of the Churches of Christ in the United States of America. Used by permission. All rights reserved.

Every reasonable effort has been made to determine copyright holders of excerpted materials and to secure permissions as needed. If any copyrighted materials have been inadvertently used in this work without proper credit being given in one form or another, please notify Our Sunday Visitor in writing so that future printings of this work may be corrected accordingly.

Our Sunday Visitor Publishing Division
Our Sunday Visitor, Inc.
200 Noll Plaza
Huntington, IN 46750
1-800-348-2440

ISBN: 978-1-68192-333-8 (Inventory No. T2017)
1. RELIGION—Biblical Studies—Bible Study Guides. 2. RELIGION—Christian Life—Spiritual Growth. 3. RELIGION—Christianity—Catholic

eISBN: 978-1-68192-334-5
LCCN: 2019943195

Cover and interior design: Lindsey Riesen
Cover art: The Crosiers

PRINTED IN THE UNITED STATES OF AMERICA

A LIFE OF CONVERSION

MEETING CHRIST IN THE GOSPELS

DEREK ROTTY

Our Sunday Visitor
Huntington, Indiana

To my beautiful wife, Khira, who has walked the path of conversion with me and aided my conversion all along the way

CONTENTS

CONTENTS

AN INVITATION TO CONVERSION

At the beginning of Mark's Gospel, Jesus immediately offers an invitation to follow him (1:14–15). If we want to answer the Lord's invitation, we must convert. This means allowing our minds and hearts to be turned more fully toward Jesus and the ideal he has for our individual lives. The Latin verb *convertere*, from which we derive the word "conversion," literally means "to turn around, to transform." Christianity requires constant, daily turning to Jesus and becoming more like him. For this reason, conversion is not just a beginning point, it is the hallmark of the Christian life.

It is far too easy to think of conversion as a moment in our past life that changed everything but requires nothing (or at least very little) of us now. Real conversion, though — repenting of sin, and turning our minds and hearts fully toward God — is not a one-time event. It is a process: One that is essential to living as Christians, to becoming more like Jesus.

Many of us can look back at a specific point in our lives when we first encountered Jesus Christ and realized his plan for us. This has been true in my own life. When I found the fullness of Christianity, the Catholic faith, at the age of twenty-two, I thought I was all set. Was I ever wrong! More than fifteen years after I was received home into the Catholic Church, I realize that the Lord wants me to become more like him every day. And I am still so far from the ideal he has for me. The Lord is still working on me, converting me every single day.

This is true for all of us as Christian disciples. Every day we face countless temptations to turn back to our selfish, materially focused way of living. All of us have our own unique temptations and pet sins that God is still helping us work through. Faced with the difficulties and frustrations of daily life, it's far too easy to turn inward and focus on ourselves. We must make a conscious effort to turn our mind and heart toward the King, our King, every day.

We become more like Jesus only over time and only if we consistently respond with a generous "yes" to the grace he offers to us. Every person who has encountered Jesus Christ, experienced initial conversion, and chosen to follow him needs to encounter him again and again. Every day our minds and hearts need to be turned more fully toward the Lord, and we need to access the grace he desires to give us.

To do this, we need to encounter Jesus each day. We need to come face to face with the Lord, who always gives his disciples an invitation to come closer, to take the next step. Even if we have had powerful experiences of God in the past, it doesn't mean that he is done with us. God *always* has more to give us.

Don't get me wrong: This is not easy. It takes effort to believe that ongoing conversion is necessary and possible. It takes a whole lot of patience before we see much measurable progress. Still, entering upon a life of conversion is eminently worth it. There is nothing more satisfying than to be in full communion with the King of the universe!

One of the best ways to encounter Jesus and continue living out conversion every day is by reading, studying, and praying with Scripture, especially the Gospels. This is why Pope Emeritus Benedict XVI has said that familiarity with Scripture will be the key to a new spiritual springtime in the Church and the world. Reading the words of Jesus and pondering the stories he told allows us to respond as the first disciples did, by turning our lives over to him.

In fact, the more we study the Gospels, the more we see that Jesus is constantly calling us to conversion, not just once, but again and again. In fact, his whole public ministry is one big invitation to conversion! Sometimes the invitation is obvious, as in the call of Matthew (Levi), the tax collector (Mt 9:9–13; Mk 2:13–17; Lk 5:27–32). At other times, we must read and ponder more deeply. Jesus tells his disciples that he teaches in parables so people might "hear with their ears, and understand with their heart, and turn for me to heal them" (Mt 13:15; see also Mk 4:12).

Jesus calls each of his potential disciples to conversion, and that call is for us too. Yes, the scriptural stories of in-person encounters with Jesus happened some two thousand years ago, and they were deeply personal. But they are recorded in Scripture for a reason. Entering into these stories allows us to turn more fully toward the Lord and advance in the life of discipleship, inviting the Lord to convert our hearts.

This book is an extended invitation to engage in *lectio divina* (divine reading). In *lectio divina*, a person asks God to allow the Scripture passage to be opened more fully, deeply, and even personally. In these pages, we will approach several Gospel passages, asking God to allow us to see them with new eyes and hear them with new ears. We will consider several individuals and the encounters with Jesus that changed their lives. I hope that these pages will offer you an opportunity to encounter Jesus, whether for the first time or in a new way, and to continue on the way of conversion in your own life.

It is also my hope that this book will be used in small groups and Bible studies. The reality is that our ongoing conversion happens within strong Christian community. Jesus never intended for us to walk this road of conversion and Christianity by ourselves. Christian disciples keep each other on the straight and narrow (sometimes hard) path. This book, therefore, includes questions at the end of each chapter for deeper discussion and understanding.

All of this leads us to know what the Bible means when it says that "the word of God is living and active" (Heb 4:12). Being immersed in the living word of God, individually and in community, gives us inspiration to follow Jesus more closely every day. I hope that by engaging in this study you will experience deeper conversion and a new zeal for the Christian life. And I hope that you will find a greater ability to share your story, your ongoing encounter with Jesus, with others.

QUESTIONS FOR DEEPER
UNDERSTANDING AND REFLECTION

1. What is your understanding of conversion? How does it apply to your life today?

2. Do you agree that conversion is the hallmark of the Christian life? Why or why not?

3. Aside from those listed, can you think of other episodes in the Gospel that make a clear call to conversion?

4. Describe a time when you encountered Jesus in a real way that has transformed you.

Chapter 1

BEYOND THE
COMMANDMENTS

Prayerfully read Matthew 19:16–22

The commandments are the basic requirements for living in right relationship with God. Salvation history makes it clear that abiding by the commandments is the path to a good life. On the other hand, refusal or failure to keep the commandments has grave consequences for our life and relationship with God.

The Old Testament abounds with examples. When Israel begins to stray from God's plan, the Lord sends prophets to call the nation back to him. And they do not merely proclaim obedience to the commandments. The prophets tell Israel, and us as well, about the Lord's deepest desires for our lives. For example, the prophet Hosea speaks on God's behalf: "For I desire mercy and not sacrifice, the knowledge of God, rather than burnt offerings" (Hos 6:6). God's will for those in relationship with him goes far beyond the commandments. He wants to give us something more, something deeper, that leads to abundant life. He wants to give us himself.

The commandments are important, not for themselves, but because they free us to grow in right relationship with the Lord, every day. In the Gospel of Matthew, Jesus makes it clear that conversion for his disciples goes beyond merely keeping the commandments. A young man approaches Jesus, asking about the way to inherit eternal life. Jesus responds, "If you would enter life, keep the commandments" (Mt 19:16–17). The young man immediately replies, "Which?" Apparently, he thinks there might be a specific formula of commandment-keeping that will be more effective than others.

In answer, Jesus lists some, but not all, of the commandments, seemingly at random. Clearly, he is indicating that all the commandments together should be kept faithfully. There is no magic formula. From first to last, all the commandments are bound up together.

Like this young man, I used to think that I could work my way to right relationship with God. If I could just do a little more of this, or a little less of that, I could earn abundant life. While I knew what was good and right (thanks to my parents and church community), somewhere along the way I began to think I had to somehow provide it for myself. I forgot that grace always leads the way.

I have known a lot of others who have fallen into this trap as well. Too many well-intentioned Christians forget that God leads and we follow. For some reason, most (maybe all) of us want to be do-it-yourself saints. So we focus on the commandments and the precepts of the Church as ends in themselves. We end up thinking, "I haven't committed adultery, and I gave my tithe to the parish, so I must be doing pretty well in the spiritual life." But the commandments aren't ends in themselves. They're only meant to lead us to Jesus Christ, who sets us free to love and serve God wholeheartedly.

This is why I've chosen to begin this book with the cautionary tale of the rich young man. That young man didn't think he needed to convert, because he kept the commandments well. How many of us think that same thing? Lots of people, even nonreligious people, fulfill the commandments. Coming to abundant life requires each of us to realize that Jesus is calling us deeper into a lifelong pilgrimage with him. This lifelong pilgrimage may include some difficulties, some getting beyond comfort zones. But it's an invitation to something much more fulfilling. If we think differently about conversion, if we think that it leads us deeper into the reality of Jesus' life, then our own life will be far more fulfilled than by merely keeping the commandments.

The young man in the Gospel replies, "All these I have observed." Yet he clearly has some intuition that something is missing from his life. Keeping the law isn't enough. So he asks, "what do I still lack?" (Mt 19:20).

This is what Jesus has come to reveal: The old covenants were preparing the people for the full revelation of God, which is Jesus himself. Following the commandments alone doesn't lead to perfection. Only the self-giving love of Jesus Christ, manifest in the new and everlasting covenant, has that power. Disciples in every era have felt this same reality. Simply obeying and keeping the commandments doesn't provide the fullness of life that we desire. We know that we are made for more, and it is turning toward Jesus more fully each day that will bring this fullness of joy into our lives.

Perfection

Jesus begins his answer to the young man with a powerful phrase: "If you would be perfect ... " (Mt 19:21). It's not enough to be a "good person." Jesus calls us to perfection. Because he calls us to it (and he will not ask anything of us that we cannot do), we know that perfection is possible. And because of the primacy of grace, we know that Jesus also gives us an effective way to attain perfection. It is beyond anything that simply keeping the commandments can bring into our lives.

It is important to note here a passage that occurs in Mark's account of this encounter of the rich young man with Jesus. Before Jesus' comment about perfection, Mark writes, "And Jesus looking upon him loved him" (Mk 10:21). Matthew does not include this detail, but I think it is important to consider, because it shows that this is an intimate moment of encounter for the young man. It should be an intimate moment of encounter for us too. We should see ourselves as the one whom Jesus looks upon with love.

Jesus then tells the young man to "go, sell what you possess and give to the poor ... and come, follow me" (Mt 19:21). If we want to become perfect, if we want to live well as disciples, we must be free from anything that possesses and controls us. For most of us, this won't mean selling everything we own.[1] What it means is keeping our possessions in their proper place. We must ask if there is anything that is keeping us from loving and relating to God fully. If there is, we must prayerfully ask the Lord how he desires for us to be rid of that thing.

Note that the Greek word that is translated into English as "what you possess" is *hyparchonta*. In ancient Greek language and culture, this word does not refer to material possessions. It refers instead to what has power over us, the things that cause us to be in the state we are. Interestingly, it is also the word for an army lieutenant.[2] Jesus does not mean just material possessions, but anything that has control over the young man. For us, this makes the lesson very clear: We can only turn more fully toward Jesus if we free ourselves from the things that have power over us. These could be material goods, physical pleasure, food, or certain vices, especially pride. No matter what our attachments are, they have to go! That is the only way for us to be free to cling to Jesus and let him provide all that we need.

What is your *hyparchonta*? What things in your life, physical or not, possess and control you? For me, the most significant temptation is my drive for knowledge. This leads to pride, and it has often come at the expense of deeper relationships with people in my life, even my own family. For others, the attachment could be money, sex, or a degraded self-image. Like the young man in this Gospel passage, each of us must decide if we will make the decision to be free of what controls us.[3]

Where do we go from here?

We know the end of this Gospel story: The young man leaves in sorrow because he is not willing to detach from his many possessions. He wants to keep living life as he always has. He is not interested in conversion because he does not want to get rid of his attachments.

When Jesus gives us the invitation to follow him, how will we choose? Are we ready and willing to turn from our current direction and follow Jesus' way? Hopefully, with his grace, we will respond rightly and take the first — or the next — step toward the abundant life that God has in store for us.

Pope Saint John Paul II, in his great teaching letter about the moral life, *Veritatis Splendor* (*VS*), focuses on this Gospel passage. Modern culture asks deep questions about good and evil, but focusing on rules and regulations cannot provide answers that satisfy our deepest longings. Instead, "People today need to turn to Christ once again in order to receive from him the answer to their questions about what is good and what is evil" (*VS* 8).

Our actions and choices are good only when they are directed toward our proper end, which is communion within God himself. The rich young man lived in a morally good way, but he lacked direction. Jesus wanted to provide him direction, and he wants to do the same for our lives, but we must commit to following him on the journey. The rich young man refused to make that commitment, and he went away sad.

The primacy of grace

It is only in turning toward Jesus that we can keep the commandments. Here is the principle that operates underneath everything else: the primacy of grace. We are not created with the natural ability to bring joy, peace, and communion into our own lives. These come only as gifts of God, and original sin makes it difficult for us to attain these realities. "This vocation to eternal life is supernatural," and it "depends entirely on God's gratuitous initiative." It exceeds the power of any creature (*Catechism of the Catholic Church* 1998). Grace makes possible what is otherwise impossible!

Our desire to repent, turn toward God, and live in right relationship with him is already a work of grace. Only by God's grace do we know our need to seek him. Saint Augustine writes in his treatise *De natura et gratia* (On Nature and Grace):

> Indeed we also work, but we are only collaborating with God who works, for his mercy has gone before us. It has gone before us so that we may be healed, and follows us so that once healed, we may be given life; it goes before us so that we may be called, and follows us so that we may be glorified; it goes before us so that we may live devoutly, and follows us so that we may always live with God: for without him we can do nothing.

God will fulfill our desire to know and follow him, because he is the only one who can fulfill it, and he wants to fulfill it.

Jesus Christ is the fulfillment of all commandments. Jesus Christ is the culmination and focal point of the heavenly Father's revelation to us. God wants a relationship with us that goes above and beyond simply keeping the commandments. We must keep the commandments, of course, but we must go beyond them if we want the abundant life that Jesus offers.

Jesus is the personification of grace, of God's free initiative to save us, redeem us, and give us abundant life. It all happens through Jesus! To find that life, we must hold fast to Jesus himself, "partaking of his life and his destiny, sharing in his free and loving obedience to the Father" (*VS* 19). That's another way of saying, "Come, follow me," as Jesus said many times in the Gospels. This starts with the commandments, but it goes much further than that. If we accept his invitation, he will lead us, by his grace, into his own perfect happiness — into beatitude.

Thankfully, not all encounters with Jesus end as the encounter with the rich young man did. The young man rejected Jesus' invitation, but we do not have to make that same choice. Instead, we can choose to reverse the young man's "no" with our own "yes."

Throughout this book, we will reflect on several other Gospel episodes in which men and women responded with a "yes" to the call of Christ and chose to follow him more deeply.

I hope each of these stories will provide you with inspiration and encouragement to answer Jesus' invitation as the rich young man could not. As you reflect on these Gospel encounters, ask the Holy Spirit to guide you more and more deeply into a life of ongoing conversion. Even if you have previously chosen the path of the rich young man, Jesus Christ always offers another opportunity. Choose, today, to follow Jesus on the path to perfect happiness and fulfillment.

QUESTIONS FOR DEEPER UNDERSTANDING AND REFLECTION

1. In your own words, define and describe grace.

2. How do you view the importance of rules and commandments in the Christian life? How has your view impacted the way you live out your faith?

3. Are there particular commandments you struggle to keep in your effort to walk more closely with Jesus?

4. What is your *hyparchonta*? What might God be asking you to give up so that you can follow him more fully?

Chapter 2

AWARENESS, REPENTANCE, AND RECONCILIATION

Prayerfully read Luke 15:11–32

During his public ministry, Jesus taught in parables. Parables are stories that engage interest and teach lessons through the details, images, and trends of daily life within a culture. Among Jesus' many parables, the parable of the prodigal son stands out as a paradigm of conversion. We might also call it the parable of the loving father, or the parable of two sons. Even though it is a story and not an encounter with Jesus during his public ministry, it is still good to consider because it provides us with deep insights into important aspects of conversion.

We know and love this story so well, probably because we all see a little bit of ourselves in each of the characters. Each of us has been like the younger son, saying hurtful things and squandering the inheritance we receive from our families and our Church. Each of us has probably been like the older son, refusing to enter into a relationship with someone because we wanted them to receive "justice," not mercy. Each of us has many opportunities to be like the loving father, waiting eagerly for reconciliation with a family member or friend despite the deep hurt they have caused us. In each of these scenarios, there is a lesson for us as we seek to enter more deeply into a life of ongoing conversion.

A troubled history

Parables have many layers of meaning. Here, the first layer of meaning is God's plan for his whole kingdom. In this story, Jesus provides an allegorical account of Israel's sordid history. A man has two sons, one of whom demands his inheritance and leaves home for "a far country" (Lk 15:11–13). Jesus intends to teach his audience about the ways that Israel has rejected the Father's perfect plan over the centuries. Jesus tells the parable so that we, too, can remember the Father's great blessings and so that we will not leave for "a far country" in our modern age.

After the reigns of King David and King Solomon, the high point of Israel's history, around the eighth century BC, the kingdom split into two because of a feud between Solomon's sons. The descendants of the ten northern tribes became the kingdom of Israel, while the descendants of the two southern tribes became the kingdom of Judah. After more than 200 years of civil and social strife, and ignoring messages from prophets, both kingdoms were exiled to the "far countries" of Assyria and Babylon. While they were exiled in Assyria, the descendants of the ten northern tribes of Israel began to worship idols and abandoned the one true God.[4]

After the period of exile, only the southern kingdom of Judah returned to the promised land. The ten northern tribes assimilated into the cultures of the surrounding nations. Like the younger son in the parable, they squandered their inheritance from the Lord by rejecting his perfect plan for them.

In the parable, the older son is bitter about the father's mercy toward the younger son. This is a bit like the way the descendants of the kingdom of Judah felt toward the descendants of the kingdom of Israel. By the time of Christ, the Samaritans were the remnant of those tribes. After several centuries of life and culture divorced from covenant relationship with God, the Samaritans were a sort of religious half-breed.[5] They wanted to mix the worship of the one true God with the beliefs and rituals of the surrounding pagan nations. This caused the Jews to view them as traitors to the covenant. Elsewhere in the Gospels, we read that "Jews have no dealings with Samaritans" (Jn 4:9). By interacting with Samaritans and sinners, Jesus wants to show that God wants his lost tribes restored to full relationship and status in his kingdom.

This is where the parable of the prodigal son comes into play. God has a plan for his new people, the Church, too. Yet many of us have rejected his will and strayed from his divine plan, sometimes causing others to stray too. Because of this, we are always in need of conversion, as has been true of God's people in every age of salvation history. The only way for the whole people of God to be fully in right relationship with him is for each of us to return to him day after day, season after season. We can find inspiration for that conversion when we read parables such as this. In fact, that's why Jesus told these parables: so we can constantly find inspiration to begin anew, despite our selfish ways. We realize too that the conversion of the whole Church happens only when each individual — you and I — convert more fully to the Lord's plan.

Seeing myself in the son

I mentioned that the first layer of meaning in the parable was historical. The parables can also be read morally (how they teach us to act) and anagogically (how they teach us about eschatological realities, the things that will come about at the end of history). The remainder of our discussion of this parable will focus primarily on the moral sense.

From the very beginning of the parable, we sense that something is amiss in the dynamics of this family. An inheritance only passes from father to son when the father dies. So when the younger son demands his inheritance, what he means is, "Father, you are dead to me."

This raises a number of questions for us. First, have I ever treated my father (or any person of importance in my life) the way the son treats his father in this story? If I had a son who treated me this way, how would I react? Would I be very hurt? Would I react as any rational human being might and reject the demand? At certain points in my life, my relationship with my father was incredibly strained. Both of us said and did hurtful things. At one point, we didn't speak for many months while I went on living with my self-righteous attitude. Only now, as a father of sons myself, can I imagine the anguish and pain I caused my father. Yet, the loving father in the parable simply "divided his living" between the sons (Lk 15:12). One note about biblical translation is interesting here. The word translated as "living" is the Greek word *bios*. That is also the Greek word for life — human life.[6] The use of this word in the parable implies that what is divided is more than simply an income or a trust fund. The father's very life is torn in two. Half of his heart has been taken from him. Or more accurately, he gives away half of his heart to the younger son.

Just think about the love our heavenly Father has for each of us. How many times, out of pride or greed or lust or anger, have we acted in ways that tore his fatherly heart in two? Jesus Christ, upon his crucifixion, had his very heart pierced, and blood and water flowed out. One of the greatest, most popular devotions that we have in the Church today is the devotion to the Sacred Heart of Jesus, in which we come to know his pierced heart more fully, even sharing in Jesus' suffering. When we enter into the heart of Jesus and the love of our heavenly Father, we can recognize the ways that we have chosen ourselves over God's more perfect plan, and that awareness enables us to change.

A far country

The younger son gathers his belongings and begins his journey into a "far country," where he "squandered his property in loose living" (Lk 15:13). This "far country" is not simply geographical. It is emotional and spiritual as well. Because of his hardness of heart, this son moves away from his loving father emotionally, intellectually, and spiritually. He squanders everything because he doesn't recognize that it has been a gift from his father.

How many of us have acted in this way throughout our lives? Because of the sinfulness that dwells in us, it is easy for us to take off for that far country, away from our heavenly Father, and to squander the gifts that he has granted to us, because we are seeking pleasure or power or both.

After squandering his inheritance, the son "began to be in want" because of a great famine (Lk 15:14). What have we done in our lives that has left us hungry for better things, hungry for the solid things that God provides instead of what the world provides? Have we found ourselves trying to fill our deep spiritual hunger with the wrong things?

One of the most poignant passages of the whole parable comes next: "So he went and joined himself to one of the citizens of that country" (Lk 15:15). This young man left his father's house and became a resident of a far country. What "far country" now claims our allegiance? To what "far countries" have we wandered at other points in our life, and what was the result? During my college years, I "joined myself" to a fraternity. After living that lifestyle with gusto, I found myself in an intellectual, emotional, and spiritual famine. I had squandered the great gift that my heavenly Father had given me.

In the parable, the citizens of the far country clearly do not treat the young man well. He is sent to feed the swine. For a Jewish person hearing this parable, this detail would have been startling, because swine symbolized everything that was unclean for Jews. While the young man feeds the swine, he is so hungry that he would eat the pigs' food if he could. He has fallen as far as possible from right relationship with his father into all that is unclean and degrading.

Although he is hungry and would eat anything, "no one gave him anything" (Lk 15:16). He has been abandoned by the citizens of this far country. He has no community; he is lonely. The fact that loneliness and isolation are prevalent here only exacerbates the problem of famine that the country faces. Physical want and need, as well as feeling alone, always seem to make moral depravity more acute. This is true in our own situation too. Things feel worse when we are hungry or tired or, especially, when we are lonely. Isolation takes away our hope, which is forged and strengthened by communal relationships.

Note the contrast between the father of the parable, who gave a large inheritance even though his son disowned him, and the citizens of the far country who now give him nothing even though he has "joined himself" to them. The father in this parable gives us a glimpse into the way our heavenly Father loves us. He showers good gifts upon us, even when we don't return his love. On the other hand, the citizens of the world have nothing substantial to offer us, and they will exploit everything we have.

Up from the bottom

Only when he hits rock bottom does conversion begin for this young man. In the next verse, we read that "he came to himself" (Lk 15:17). This is a moment of *metanoia*, a turning of the mind. He comes face to face with himself.[7] He must recognize, in his mind first and then in his heart, that he has had a terrible attitude and acted in ways that have harmed him and his closest relations. Without this moment, the son cannot acknowledge the wrong that he has committed.

For every person, there is at least one significant moment when he realizes that he has sinned and strayed far from the heavenly Father's plan for his life. Yet, in the life of ongoing conversion, our understanding of this reality deepens over time because the grace of God brings us face to face with ourselves time and time again.

In the same verse, the son thinks to himself, "How many of my father's hired servants have bread enough and to spare, but I perish here with hunger!" (Lk 15:17). He decides that it is better for him to return to his father's house, even as a slave, than to remain in this far country. In the house of a loving father, even a slave is a son. That is why this young man is willing to say,

"Father, I have sinned against heaven and before you; I am no longer worthy to be called your son; treat me as one of your hired servants" (Lk 15:18–19).

At this point, the son decides to rise and go to his father. He is no longer just thinking about it. He has decided to act, as each of us must decide and act. In the ongoing way of conversion, we must continually decide how we will return to the love of the heavenly Father, and we must carry out those decisions with courage and conviction.

The suffering love of the father

While the son treks back to his father's house, his father sees him coming, and the parable tells us he "had compassion" (Lk 15:20). The father has been suffering too because of this strained relationship. More than that, he has been watching for his estranged son. We can imagine the father gazing out the window, just waiting for his beloved son to return. The father's suffering shows us that there is no way to have compassion unless we too have suffered. The word compassion means "to suffer with." It is sad, but beautiful: The father and the son have been suffering together, from different sides, throughout this estrangement. That is precisely why the father "ran and embraced him and kissed him" (Lk 15:20). The father waited, not with pride, but with a longing to have a restored relationship with his son, at any cost.

"Father," says the son, "I have sinned against heaven and before you; I am no longer worthy to be called your son" (Lk 15:21). The son knows that he cannot simply ignore his wrongdoing. He has to face it and admit it. For us as members of the Church, this happens in the Sacrament of Reconciliation. This sacrament is crucial for the ongoing process of conversion. Naming our sins in the sacrament, and bringing them back as often as necessary, allows us to submit them to God's grace and allows us to continue to grow.

Before I was received fully into the Catholic Church, I never named a specific sin against God; I only asked generically for forgiveness. I have realized, over the years, that naming specific sins brings a necessary level of accountability for cutting out those habits from my life. When I confess specific sins, even if they are small, I begin searching my conscience for more serious sins so I can get those out too.

The best news of all for the son in the parable is that his father does not want him back in any diminished capacity. He wants his son in a fully restored, right relationship, complete with robe, ring, sandals, and a great banquet (Lk 15:22–23). The celebration can commence because a son has returned to life. This is true of our relationship with the heavenly Father too. He longs for us to be restored, no matter how we may have rejected his loving plan. We are worth being restored to our place in his plan as royal heirs. There is much rejoicing in heaven every time we turn back from our sinful ways, our egotistical trip into the far country of sin.

Generosity, not jealousy

The story doesn't end with the festival, however. The elder son is jealous of the father's mercy and generosity. He wants to know why he has not received a fattened calf and a festival, since he has always done his duty to the father. It even seems that the elder son wants nothing to do with the celebration for his younger brother. He does not want to participate in the joyful moment.

There is ample opportunity for personal reflection here, especially for those of us who have committed our lives to Christ and his Church. Have we ever been angry about God's mercy toward others, thinking they didn't deserve it? Are we holding a grudge against someone who has left our side and chosen to squander good things? The heavenly Father's mercy goes far beyond our faulty human reason. Instead, it is based on sheer, undying love.

I find that I often react like the older son. I want to place conditions on God's mercy. I think particularly of people who have harmed me unjustly, or broken relationship with me like the younger son did with the father in the parable. I want justice. I want those people to apologize for their wrongdoing. Yet mercy is far greater than justice. God's mercy is infinite, and I am called to imitate him.

The parable does not tell us whether the older son chooses to enter into the celebration or if he chooses to remain outside. His father invites him in, and that is all we know. Here we see how Scripture is "living and active" (Heb 4:12). It invites us into the mystery as a participant. We do not know what the older son chooses because, in the life of grace, we are the older son, and we still have to choose how to react when the Lord calls us to exercise a joyful mercy. The parable doesn't have a clear ending because we are the ending, and we have to make a choice. Will we choose to imitate the Lord's generous mercy?

QUESTIONS FOR DEEPER UNDERSTANDING AND REFLECTION

1. Why do you think this parable is so central to Christian spirituality? Why is it so beloved by many?

2. Which title of the parable most resonates with you: the parable of the prodigal son, the parable of the loving father, or the parable of the two sons? Why?

3. Have you ever treated someone close to you as the younger son treated his father? Have you ever strained or ended relationships out of pride or any other serious sin? What happened, and where does that relationship stand now?

4. Have you ever found yourself in a "far country," away from God and the Church? What caused you to realize this? How did you react once you realized it?

5. What does the unconditional love and mercy of the heavenly Father mean to you? How would you express it to others?

6. Do you find that there is some of the older son's tendency in you too? Why or why not?

Chapter 3

THE EUCHARIST

Prayerfully read Luke 24:13–35

It may seem counterintuitive to move ahead to the very end of the Gospel narrative at this point in our study. However, with all that we have stated about grace, we would be remiss if we moved forward without considering the avenue of grace par excellence in the Christian life: the Eucharist, which is the Body, Blood, Soul, and Divinity of Jesus himself; which we receive as our food, and is thus our supreme source of grace.

Our Catholic Faith teaches us that the Eucharist is "the source and summit of the Christian life." Indeed, every part of our faith, including prayers, works of ministry, and apostolic life, is "bound up with the Eucharist and are oriented toward it" (CCC 1324). Saint Peter Julian Eymard teaches us even more fervently in his classic treatise on the Most Blessed Sacrament: "Since we have in Holy Communion the grace, the model, and the practice of all the virtues, all of them finding their exercise in this divine action, we shall profit more by Communion than by all other means of sanctification. But to that end, Holy Communion must become the thought that dominates mind and heart. It must be the aim of all study, of piety, of the virtues."

The simple reality is that we can't do Christian life without the Eucharist. For this reason, we are going to cover it now, before moving on to other ways in which Christ seeks to encounter us.

Countless conversions (and reversions) to Jesus Christ have happened over twenty centuries because of the Eucharist. Obviously, there is a powerful draw to this reality that is Jesus' Body, Blood, Soul, and Divinity — the same Body, Blood, Soul, and Divinity that walked the earth some two thousand years ago. This is precisely what drew me finally and fully into the Catholic Church, and I'll tell you more of that story as we walk through this chapter. There is one episode in the Gospels, though, that seems to capture this reality more effectively than any other: the events that took place on the road to Emmaus.

The Resurrection and the Eucharist

"That very day two of them were going to a village named Emmaus, about seven miles from Jerusalem" (Lk 24:13). The first three words should cause our ears to perk up. Remember, the evangelists (the authors of the Gospel texts) don't waste words. So when Luke writes, "That very day," he means something specific. Which day is it? It is the day of the Resurrection.

This reveals something about the intimate connection between the Resurrection and the Eucharist. These connections also crop up in other important aspects of our faith. For example, Jesus said at the Last Supper: "This is my body" (Lk 22:19), he was referring to not only his Body sacrificed on the cross, but also his resurrected, glorified Body. Another example is that adults who are received into the Catholic Church generally receive their first holy Communion at the Easter Vigil Mass, the holiest Mass of the year, when Catholics imitate the disciples waiting for the Resurrection. In fact, each Sunday Eucharist (indeed, every Eucharist) is a celebration of the Resurrection.

I have heard it taught (rightly so) that we should approach every Eucharist as if it is our first and our last. I remember well the Easter Vigil at which I was received into the Catholic Church and received the Eucharist for the first time. At that moment, my Lord united himself to me in the most intimate way possible in this life. The only way I can be more intimate with him is in heaven. This is true every time we receive the Eucharist. Knowing this can help keep us in the right frame of mind as we approach this sacrament, which is the be-all and end-all of our faith.

The hidden Jesus

In the next verses of the Gospel passage, we read that these two men are "talking with each other about all these things that had happened" (Lk 24:14). It is interesting to observe that if they are talking about the life, ministry, and death of Jesus, then they certainly are gathered in the Lord's name. In another Gospel passage, Jesus promises to be among us when we gather in his name (Mt 18:20). So, while they are talking and discussing together, "Jesus himself drew near and went with them" (Lk 24:15).

Even though these men don't yet know that it is Jesus who has joined them on the journey, this moment provides an opportunity for deeper discipleship and understanding. This proves the principle of grace at work: God is always moving first, looking for opportunities to draw near to us, before we ever even think to respond to him.

Here the Gospels reveal another powerful reality: "But their eyes were kept from recognizing him" (Lk 24:16). Revelation happens in God's way, in God's time, according to his grace. Of course, there are things we can do to dispose ourselves to receive him, and maybe these disciples weren't quite disposed, but no one can force it. Augustine even tells us that their eyes were prevented from recognizing Jesus because the Lord didn't want them to see him yet. He wanted them to know him at a later moment, which we'll get to shortly.

It is important to ask ourselves: How many times have my own eyes been kept from recognizing Jesus in the ordinary movements of my life? Where has God been preparing me, in his own perfect plan, for an encounter that would be all the more powerful later on?

Along these lines, I think of my own relationship with the Catholic Church and the Mass. I grew up in a rural area where the Catholic Church was not at all part of the religious and cultural landscape. I knew only two Catholics, and I found out about one of them only during high school. It was not until I was a young adult, ready to ask significant questions about religion, that the Lord opened my eyes by putting Catholics in my path to help lead me to the Church and the Eucharist. It's not that I couldn't have seen before, but I probably couldn't have seen so clearly the beauty that is present in the Catholic Church.

When Jesus joins the disciples on their journey to Emmaus, he begins by asking what they're talking about. The Gospels tell us that "they stood still, looking sad" (Lk 24:17). Of course, Jesus already knows what they're talking about, and he knows that they are sad. But they don't know that he knows. He enters into their sadness and walks the journey with them. Thus he exhibits the most effective method of ministry and evangelization: Enter into people's lives, including their pains. Walk with them. Get to know their stories. That will be the opportunity to bring them deeper into the Christian mystery, to assist the Lord in bringing them to conversion, and to turn that pain into burning zeal and joy.

Jesus "plays dumb" when these disciples question him about his whereabouts in recent days. Basically, he says to them, "Tell me what's been going on in Jerusalem, since you think I don't know." The disciples' answer indicates that they were expecting a messiah to restore political power to Israel — a common expectation among the Jewish people at that time. Apparently they had not listened or believed when Jesus clearly taught that his redemptive mission was quite different. Throughout his preaching ministry, Jesus had been open with his disciples about his mission: He told them it would involve suffering and the sacrifice of the cross. Yet he also assured them it would be marked by his Resurrection after three days (Mt 16:21). Here again, grace is guiding the way. God's perfect design was them was to have this beautiful experience on the road to Emmaus.

Knowing his story

The Resurrection and the Eucharist were so real to Luke and the rest of the Christian community that the Gospel writer was willing to stake their reputation on witnesses that ancient authorities would have dismissed: women.

The disciples on the way to Emmaus tell their mysterious friend: "Moreover, some women of our company amazed us. They were at the tomb early in the morning and ... said that he was alive" (Lk 24:22–23). Women are the first eyewitnesses to the Resurrection. This was definitely countercultural during that period in Roman and Jewish history. Women were not viewed as credible witnesses, yet Luke depended on them to make his case for this most important miracle of Jesus Christ. As Christians today, are we similarly convinced about the reality of the Resurrection and the Eucharist?

Finally, the disciples tell Jesus about the apostles' reaction to the women's news. They "went to the tomb, and found it just as the women had said; but him they did not see" (Lk 24:24). At this point, they believe, but they are still clearly confused by the whole event, primarily because they had been thinking in a totally different direction.

Now Jesus begins to speak: "O foolish men, and slow of heart to believe all that the prophets have spoken! Was it not necessary that the Christ should suffer these things and enter into his glory?" (Lk 24:25–26). Here Jesus lets them know that they should have been paying closer attention all along. If they had, these realities that have come to pass might make more sense. Yet for whatever reason, they weren't ready to receive fully what God had to offer them until now, even though they had heard Jesus' teachings.

God's grace operates in God's time, which is very different from our own expectations. God working on his own, often seemingly slow timeline helps in the life of ongoing conversion. We turn toward the Lord in small steps, responding to the small amounts of grace we can handle at one time. The disciples took the huge step of following Jesus, but their process of conversion would take place over the rest of their lives. The same is true for us today.

Now at last, the disciples on the road to Emmaus are ready for Jesus to bring them deeper into his great mystery. "And beginning with Moses and all the prophets, he interpreted to them in all the Scriptures the things concerning himself" (Lk 24:27). In other words, Jesus offers them the best Bible study in history. This single verse and the principle that it illustrates tell us that understanding the story of Sacred Scripture is essential to meeting and knowing Jesus fully. If we meet Jesus fully in the Eucharist, as Catholics believe, then we should be prepared for such an encounter by knowing his story, which is the story of Israel laid out in the Old Testament and the story of the Church laid out in the New Testament outside the Gospels' accounts.

The exciting part is, each of us gets to participate in the "best Bible study ever" every time we attend Mass. The Mass, specifically the Liturgy of the Word, tells us again and again the powerful story of God's chosen people throughout history. Every Liturgy of the Word culminates in the Eucharistic Liturgy, where Jesus' paschal mystery is re-presented to us under the appearances of bread and wine. Throughout our lives of ongoing conversion, we should always desire to grow more deeply in communion with Jesus Christ through the Eucharist.

My own journey of conversion has borne this trait. As I have grown in my knowledge of Sacred Scripture and the teachings of the Catholic faith, my desire to receive Jesus in the Blessed Sacrament has also grown. I also have heard many people comment, as they journey through RCIA (the path by which people come into full communion with the Catholic Church), that their own study of the Bible becomes much fuller and richer when they hear of, and ultimately receive, the Eucharist.

In the breaking of the bread

These two disciples have already had a profound experience, yet their encounter with Christ is about to deepen significantly. When they reach their destination, they begged him, "Stay with us" (Lk 24:29). All of us long to remain connected when we have a satisfying experience of truth. The disciples do not yet know it is Jesus who walks with them, yet they have received a deeper taste of what awaits them, and they want to hold on to it.

The unknown traveler agrees to stay with them, and they prepare a meal. Now is the moment when Jesus can reveal fully who he is and what he has to offer his disciples. "When he was at table with them, he took the bread and blessed and broke it, and gave it to them" (Lk 24:30). Here Jesus uses the essential Eucharistic formula, instituted at the Last Supper and passed on by the ministry of the Church (1 Cor 11:23–26). For nearly two thousand years, this has been the formula by which Jesus becomes sacramentally present, coming into our midst in a real and substantial way. We ought to be continually in awe of this reality, allowing it to transform us again and again.

The Eucharistic formula makes something special happen to the disciples in Emmaus: "And their eyes were opened and they recognized him" (Lk 24:31). This is the moment, the setting in which Jesus wants to be fully known; this is the moment for which he waited to come most fully into their minds and hearts. This episode has come to its climax. An ancient poem by Saint Ephrem the Syrian captures the moment well:

> When the disciples' eyes
> were held closed
> bread too was the key
> whereby their eyes were opened
> to recognize the omniscient:
> saddened eyes beheld

a vision of joy
and were instantly filled with happiness.

(from *Hymns of Paradise*)

This short poem allows us to catch a small glimpse of what these disciples might have felt in that moment. Their dashed hopes have been restored, and they immediately know the blessed happiness that accompanies disciples who walk fully in the life of grace.

Burning within

Suddenly we are told that Jesus "vanished out of their sight" as soon as they recognized him (Lk 24:31). Where did Jesus go, and more importantly, why did he choose to vanish? I like Augustine's explanation here: "He withdrew from them in the body, since he was held by them in faith. That indeed is why the Lord absented himself in the body from the whole church, and ascended into heaven, for the building up of faith."[8] Jesus, still sacramentally present in the bread, chooses to hide himself again for one simple reason: This will allow these disciples to continue to grow in faith. This has been true down through the Christian centuries, and it still is true today. Jesus makes himself smaller and less obvious so that we can continue to be converted.

Yes, initial conversion leads us to the Eucharist, but it is equally true that the Eucharist fosters our ongoing conversion in the Christian life. There is no better way to be transformed and become more like Jesus.

After this powerful encounter, the disciples look at each other and ask, "Did not our hearts burn within us while he talked to us on the road, while he opened to us the Scriptures?" (Lk 24:32). Here they have recognized in hindsight how things have built up to this moment. The grace of a burning heart — a deep desire to know and experience truth, goodness, and beauty —

is preparation for knowing and encountering Truth, Goodness, and Beauty himself. Where do we encounter Jesus more truly and substantially than in the Eucharist? Nowhere. Our burning hearts are satisfied perfectly by Eucharistic communion because it is Jesus, truly present under the appearance of bread and wine.

A burning heart is a sign of conversion. When we experience a desire to know more about Jesus, to love others more fully, and to share the love and mercy of God, our hearts burn. Ongoing conversion means that those desires continue to deepen and grow over time.

Impelled to mission

Intimate encounters with Jesus always put us on a mission. The disciples knew this, for we read, "And they rose that same hour and returned to Jerusalem" (Lk 24:33). There are a few things that should stun us here and allow us to see how incredible this episode is. First, it is late at night. Remember, they have just been eating dinner on the day of the Resurrection. Walking on ancient roads was quite treacherous, even during daytime. To walk late at night might surely have meant inviting robbery or worse.

Besides the danger of the walk, it was not a short walk. We are told that Emmaus was about seven miles from Jerusalem. Assuming these are fit, healthy men who can walk at a decent pace, they probably would have arrived back in Jerusalem around midnight, after having walked fourteen miles that day. Yet their transformative encounter with Jesus leads to newfound dedication and a burning desire to share what they have experienced.

When they arrive in the Holy City, they find "the Eleven gathered together and those who were with them" (Lk 24:33). Here, we have a gathering of the earliest Church. What is happening at this gathering of the Church? They are recounting the amazing, unbelievable events of the day; they are proclaiming the Resurrection (Lk 24:34). They are giving testimony. Immediately, these two are invited to share with the Church their own encounter with Jesus, so "they told what had happened on the road" (Lk 24:35).

Luke concludes this episode with words that have resonated powerfully down the centuries: "how he was known to them in the breaking of the bread" (Lk 24:35). Ultimately, every story of conversion tells how we have come into deeper union with Jesus. In this case, these men have experienced the most powerful, deepest way of all. Nothing more needs to be said. If we want to turn and follow Jesus, we must seek him in the Eucharist. It is necessary for us to receive his essence into ourselves so that we might become what we consume.

QUESTIONS FOR DEEPER UNDERSTANDING AND REFLECTION

1. How has the Eucharist been a source of deeper conversion and faith for you?

2. How would you answer if someone asked you about the connection between the Eucharist and another aspect of our Catholic faith?

3. Have you ever had difficulty accepting the truth that Jesus Christ is truly, bodily present in the Eucharist? What helped you come to such faith?

4. Has there been a time when your heart burned passionately for truth, goodness, and beauty? Has the Eucharist helped you to live out your passions more fully?

5. Consider your own testimony about your faith in Jesus and the Eucharist. Are you able to share it?

Chapter 4

TRUST AND CRUCIFORMITY

Prayerfully read Luke 5:1–11

The story of Simon Peter's transformation into a disciple of Jesus and a leader of the Church spans the entire Gospel narrative. From the beginning of the Gospel stories to the end, we see that the transformation of Simon Peter's life is total. At many significant points, the fisherman is called to learn and exhibit deeper trust in the Lord's plan for him. Nowhere is that clearer than in his first encounter with Jesus, by the Sea of Galilee, with his business partners — his fellow fishermen. This episode of Simon Peter's initial conversion is marked by a radical trust, which grows for the rest of his earthly life, up to and including his martyrdom. This growing trust leads the prince of the apostles to "take up his cross daily" and follow Jesus (Lk 9:23).

Reading the story of Peter's first encounter with the Messiah should inspire us to trust Jesus more, as Peter begins to do in this scene. As we learn to trust in this way, we grow in our capacity to take up our crosses daily and follow Jesus more closely. Following the example of the first leader of the Church, we can experience the same ongoing conversion that he underwent as he continually recommitted to following Jesus.

A personal encounter

Even before Simon enters the scene, the text tells us that "the people pressed upon [Jesus] to hear the word of God" (Lk 5:1). This group of people by the Sea of Galilee want to know the revelation of God. They are excited to hear what this messianic figure has to say.

Yet the fullness of revelation will happen not only through words. Jesus shows this in a powerful way when, in response to this crowd's desire, he initiates the call of Simon to conversion. Perhaps he wants to show us that simply hearing, even knowing, the word of God may not bring us to the conversion God desires.

For that radical, ongoing conversion to happen, we must have a personal encounter with Jesus Christ.

In order to make this point abundantly clear, Jesus finds two empty boats by the lake. These two boats, we find out, belong to Simon, James, and John. The fishermen have just finished a night of fishing, without a catch, and they are "washing their nets" (Lk 5:2), tending to the mundane tasks of their livelihood, when the Lord appears in their lives. Then Jesus gets into Simon's boat (Lk 5:3) without his permission and makes a demand so that the people can hear him. Simon must be shocked at this course of events. He just wants to go home after an unsuccessful business venture. Instead, an itinerant preacher comes and makes demands on his time and resources.

Perhaps this is how Jesus has shown up in your life as well. I recall well that I was in the midst of making plans for graduate school and a professional career when Jesus called me in a way that would transform me forever. I was perfectly content making my own way in an intellectual, academic world. I never expected to be called to make a radical act of trust and follow Jesus. Yet this is how Jesus works nearly every time. Often he asks for our radical trust by radical, unexpected actions on his part. How do we react when Jesus imposes upon our goods, our gifts, or our desires? Do we complain? Do we oblige readily? To choose the latter is a sign that we are being converted, even just a little bit, toward Jesus.

Into the deep

After Jesus gets into Simon's boat, he begins to teach the crowd. This is the very first teaching from the Messiah that Simon has heard. When Jesus finishes teaching, he immediately looks toward Simon and gives a command: "Put out into the deep and let down your nets for a catch" (Lk 5:4). Jesus has revealed something, and now he turns to a specific person for a response. In this case, Jesus is looking for a response from the first leader of his college of apostles. The pattern, though, is meant for all of us as well. The Lord reveals something and then he seeks our response. He looks for our minds and hearts to be turned more fully to the truth that he makes known. This is always how he works.

Let's look at this concept through the lens of the rest of this episode on the water. Jesus commands this expert fisherman to push away from the shore and drop his nets again. Naturally, the one who is the expert retorts that he has "toiled all night and took nothing!" (Lk 5:5). Surely he has already employed every trick of the trade in order to earn a living and provide for his family. By all reasonable accounts, that should be enough to decide to pack it in and return on another day. Yet Jesus doesn't worry about any of that. A loose translation of Jesus' meaning in this whole exchange might be: "Trust me." Jesus is asking for a response of trust as the beginning of the life of conversion and discipleship. In fact, trust is the first major step of conversion. These acts of trust must happen again and again throughout our lives as we follow him.

The Latin translation of "Put out into the deep" is "*Duc in altum.*" When my wife and I honeymooned in Italy, we found beautiful crosses with this powerful inscription on their backs. We had the crosses blessed by Pope Benedict and promptly hung one in our home. Nine years later, during some very difficult circumstances, we were discerning a call to move our family to another city, far beyond our comfort zone. In the process of deciding to move, the pastor for whom I would work told me that it was an opportunity for me to put out into the deep. I knew that this was a moment when God was calling me to deeper trust in him, despite the difficulties and unknown circumstances.

Perhaps Simon realizes in this moment with Jesus that he is dealing with something more than a natural, reasonable reality. Perhaps that is the reason he makes his act of trust: "But *at your word* I will let down the nets" (Lk 5:5, emphasis added). Simon continues his fishing expedition because a little-known miracle worker tells him to do so. The process of ongoing, ever-deepening conversion always begins with a single act of trust like Simon's. In making an act of trust, my will is turned toward the one who asks for it.

The Lord's response to Simon's act of trust is overwhelmingly generous. The Lord gifts Simon and his business partners with "a great shoal of fish," so big that "their nets were breaking" (Lk 5:6). Remember, Simon is a professional fisherman. His nets are likely able to handle a large catch. Yet God's gift overwhelms Simon's capacity. This should cause each of us to realize that the grace of God is always more plentiful than any of us can ever imagine.

In response to the huge catch, Simon calls on his fellow fishermen, James and John, to assist. Everyone who witnesses this event is "astonished" along with Simon. The great catch of fish is not only God's way of honoring Simon's act of trust, it might also be God's way of "hooking" the other two fishermen into trusting him more deeply. It seems as though Jesus catches three for one in his fishing expedition here.

It is good for us to spend a moment examining one important word in the Gospel text. The Greek word that is translated as "astonished" ("amazed" in some other places in the Gospels) is *thambos*. *Thambos*, says one commentator on this passage, describes "religious awe before the Holy."[9] It also can be translated as "wonder" as in Acts 3:10.

Wonder is a foundational principle in our spiritual lives and in a life of ongoing conversion. If we lose the gift of wonder, our minds and hearts can no longer be fully immersed in God's life and love. Thankfully, wonder (also known as fear of the Lord) is one of the seven gifts of the Holy Spirit, which we receive in baptism and which is strengthened in us at confirmation. We can ask God for an increase of this gift.

On the other hand, there are ways that we risk losing wonder. Failure to enter into prayer is what most fully robs us of wonder. We can also lose wonder if we forget to look at God's glorious creation, both in nature and in humanity. Each of these moments (entering into prayer, asking for an increased gift, meeting God in creatures) provides an opportunity for conversion. When we do these again and again over the course of our lives, that is on-going conversion.

By taking time to think about what astonishes us, each of us will be brought to deeper, fuller conversion because we will know from which font we can drink most fully. Some people may be astonished at God's love as it expressed in the tender care one person provides to another. Others may be astonished at the way that God's creative work allows a beautiful garden to grow.

As I look back on my experience of and relationship with God, I can think of many times when I have been astonished and amazed, that I have stood in wonder and awe. There are the many times that God has kept me safe from harm and personal disaster resulting from bad choices in my younger days. There are the times when the Lord has provided for my family's financial needs. During my years of work in parishes, I have heard about and witnessed many miraculous healings from serious illness. I am probably most astonished by God's handiwork, though, in science and nature. I stand in awe of the amazing realities that God has ordained to inspire wonder in human beings: the physics of beautiful sunsets, the development of ancient mountain ranges, the detailed intricacy of human biology, and so on.

Simon's astonishment leads to a radical admission: "Depart from me," he exclaims, "for I am a sinful man, O Lord" (Lk 5:8). We must ask ourselves why this man who has received such a great grace wants to dismiss this Messiah from his presence. Quite often, we shrink back from the Lord's gifts and plans for us because we think we are unworthy. After this initial recognition, if we continue along the process of conversion, we continue to become more aware of our unworthiness as we grow closer to the Lord in his holiness. A life of conversion means continuing to let Jesus love us, minister to us, and heal us precisely because of our unworthiness.

The reality is that we are unworthy. We do not deserve God's grace, and we are naturally not up to the task of growing into the fullness of his desires for our lives. So, it is quite easy to desire to remain perpetually in our comfort zone, because there we will not be challenged for something greater. But this cannot be the final word. We must enter the life of conversion, always realizing that God has something more for us, that he wants to bring us deeper into his life of grace.

A change in name means a change in mission

Here it is important to note that Luke changes the name he calls the fisherman. For the first and only time in this episode, Simon is called Simon Peter. This should tell us that this moment will have a profound impact on who this fisherman is and who he will be in the future. Think about it: Every time the Lord changes a person's name in the Bible, that person is set on a new, very powerful course. Think of Jacob becoming Israel, or Saul becoming Paul. In order to signify Simon's conversion to God's plan, Jesus will tell him, "you are Peter" (Mt 16:18). Luke's use of a name change at this moment signifies the conversion that has taken place and will continue to take place throughout the next several years of Simon's life.

The good news for Simon Peter, and for us, is that Jesus does not allow potential and present disciples to remain in their comfort zones. After Simon's confession of his unworthiness, Jesus gazes upon him and says, "Do not be afraid; henceforth you will be catching men" (Lk 5:10). Throughout the Bible, the phrase

"Do not be afraid" carries a special meaning. It is always addressed to a human being as God bestows a great mission and role (*munus*, in Latin). It is always a word of encouragement for spiritual strength. Look at the stories of Judith, Tobit, Jeremiah, Ezekiel, Judas Maccabeus, Zechariah (father of John the Baptist), Mary (Jesus' mother), and Joseph (Jesus' foster father). "Do not be afraid" is intended to lift them up for the special role that God has in store for them.

This is the same for Peter. Jesus speaks a word that simultaneously provides the grace for Peter to turn away from fear of what is unknown, and to turn toward a divinely inspired mission that will have an impact on all human history. Perhaps even more than his admission of sinfulness, this is a major moment of conversion for Simon. It marks his transition from fisherman to apostle.

The Lord wants to provide such grace and conversion to each and every disciple throughout history. He wants us to know that he has a unique mission marked out for each of us, and that we should have courage amid that mission (*munus*). More than that, we should realize that God is providing the practical necessities, the stuff that we need, to be successful in our unique missions. The Lord is providing everything we need to be successful in the *munus* that he gives to us, both individually and as a Church. Along with Saint Joan of Arc, we can say, "I was born for this," and we can know that we are fulfilling God's plan for our lives.

The choice to leave everything

In response to Jesus' remark that they will be fishers of men, Simon Peter, James, and John "left everything and followed him" (Lk 5:11). This is the only suitable response to a call from Jesus. The response of these three men stands in stark contrast to the young man, studied in chapter 1, who asks about eternal life. What is the difference between these three men and the young man? The simplest explanation is that these three men have come to trust Jesus in a way that the young man did not. Remember, trust is the first important movement in a life of conversion.

And this kind of trust is not just a nice idea. It is radical, life-changing, and even a bit scary. When these three men choose to leave their boats and follow Jesus, they are making a decision that has "obvious economic and vocational [and] deep-seated social ramifications."[10] They have chosen a life of uncertainty on the fringes of society, rather than the relative security of operating a fishing business in Capernaum.

This will be a reality for us today, too, if we seek to commit our lives to Christ. It has certainly happened several times throughout my career in ministry. Jesus Christ has called me to be a minister of the Gospel, even though I might prefer the security or prestige of a life in academia. Sometimes, the hardest part is allowing the Lord to stretch my comfort zones in ministering to his people. If I were a business executive, I could make more money. If I were a university professor, I could be considered the expert in some field of study. As it is, however, God asks me to put out into the deep, a place I'm not always comfortable, and minister to people who are hurting, searching, and learning, just as I am — though I often don't realize it. Every day I have to trust that God knows better than I do what will bring me to my fullest, most perfect self. This is the kind of trust God wants from all of us as his disciples.

Cruciformity

Although it is outside this Gospel passage (and outside the whole scriptural record, actually), we must deal briefly with the result of Simon Peter's trust in Jesus. Trusting Jesus and following him leads Peter to a cross. Quite literally, Peter follows Jesus' instruction: "If any man would come after me, let him deny himself and take up his cross daily and follow me. For whoever would save his life will lose it; and whoever loses his life for my sake, he will save it" (Lk 9:23–24). After roughly thirty years of being led where he did not want to go (see Jn 21:18) and guiding the newly established Catholic Church, Peter will be crucified like Jesus, albeit upside down. Suffering this martyrdom is the full flowering of Simon Peter's act of trust in his boat on the Sea of Galilee. Ultimately, Peter's trust in Jesus will lead to him becoming like Jesus even in his death — to cruciformity.

Cruciformity, quite simply, is conformity to the cross of Jesus Christ. It is connecting to Jesus through our own sufferings. The common Catholic saying, "Offer it up," is one way of recognizing that cruciformity is necessary in the life of a Christian. Indeed, it is the pattern of the Christian life, the life of ongoing conversion.

As a result, cruciformity must be a central theme in every Christian's life, as it was in Peter's. If we choose to turn toward Jesus, follow him, and live as he directs us, we must take up our crosses. The path of the cross leads to Calvary, the place of death that brings life. This means that conversion leads to death — death to self. As Christians, we are called to die to ourselves. Perhaps we will be called to a red martyrdom (physical death and the spilling of blood for Jesus), but we definitely are called to a death to self that will glorify the Lord and lift up others. We are called to stretch out our hands (Jn 21:18) and ensure that our brothers and sisters are strengthened for this journey of Christian living (Lk 22:32).

Still, we do not need to fear. We are a people of hope, even in the face of cruciformity and death. The Resurrection comes after the cross. But what does this mean for those of us who aren't yet living in the New Jerusalem? (that's all of us). It means that we can remain hopeful and joyful even in our sufferings. It means that we can confidently expect good things to follow on the heels of situations that hurt us and test our virtue (Heb 11:1). It means that we can look for areas of consolation in our lives, even small areas, to help us through the desolations that slowly conform us to Christ — if we let them. No matter what comes, we know, from the example of Saint Peter and so many others, that the cross triumphs in the end and that the process of being conformed to the cross of Christ will lead us to eternal happiness. So let's move forward in cruciformity and in hope!

QUESTIONS FOR DEEPER
UNDERSTANDING AND REFLECTION

1. Can you describe a moment when Jesus entered or reentered your life in an unexpected way?

2. Write down or share a story about how the Lord asked you to trust him more deeply, to "put out into the deep." What was the "great catch" that he provided?

3. Who have been your greatest partners and companions in helping you to encounter the Lord more fully, to receive the fullness of his grace?

4. Has there ever been a moment when you have felt unworthy in the Lord's presence? Did you try to move away from him, or did you enter into this unknown dynamic?

5. How has the Lord astonished you? How have you been amazed at his work in your life?

6. What do you think of the reality that conversion must lead us to death to self? Where do you need to ask the Lord for greater trust that he will give you the grace to meet any challenges that arise?

Chapter 5

FREEDOM

Prayerfully read John 4:3–42

The story of the Samaritan woman at the well, told in the fourth chapter of Saint John's Gospel, is an iconic expression of conversion. Throughout Christian history, and especially in recent years, much ink has been used to comment on and illuminate this episode, and with good reason: The story has many important things to teach us. At its heart, this story is one of radical conversion that leads to newfound freedom in Jesus. And it is a story that disciples already committed to walking with Jesus can return to again and again for inspiration. At its heart, this woman's story is one of meeting the God who is constantly in search of us. No matter where we are in our life of discipleship, we must always be open to God seeking us and be ready to convert once again in response.

Divine appointment

The story opens by telling us of a divine appointment. John writes, "[Jesus] had to pass through Samaria" (Jn 4:4). Yet a few verses later, we learn that "Jews have no dealings with Samaritans" (Jn 4:9). The reality is that Jesus did not have to pass through Samaria because of convenience or social custom. In fact, just the opposite. Jews avoided Samaria because of the animosity that existed between those two peoples. Most Jews of the time would have crossed the Jordan River and traveled on the eastern banks in order to get from Jerusalem to Galilee without having to travel through Samaria.[11] Yet Jesus chooses to go through Samaria to work in a specific person's life and to teach us something specific. In other words, Jesus has to go through Samaria because he has a divine appointment there. Jesus clearly wants to bring something specific to this person and this place, despite the perceived improprieties.

This small, seemingly insignificant detail should remind us of the workings of God's grace. It often seems small and insignificant, yet we realize just how powerful it really is when it comes near to us. Moreover, we must remember that grace always comes first. By his free initiative, the Lord sets this divine appointment. He will be waiting for us when and as he knows is best.

Before we go further into this Gospel story, it is important to pause and reflect on the divine appointments in our own lives. Do you notice when the Lord sets them? I must admit that I often do not. I make schedules and stick to them rigidly. I have a certain way in my head I think life should run, and I don't always leave a lot of room for God to work in unexpected ways. That's probably why he has to break through unannounced. Yet when I do notice that God wants to engage me in a special moment, and when I'm flexible enough to follow his lead, amazing things can happen. God's providential plan always precedes our plans, and is always far better than our plans, if we give him the chance to act.

Setting the scene

Jesus has come to the field that Jacob[12] gave to his son Joseph; the field contains Jacob's well. These details shed important light on what Jesus intends to do in this meeting.

First, by making this divine appointment in a place with ties all the way back to Israel and Joseph, Jesus shows that there is something more foundational and more important than the animosity that exists between Jews and Samaritans. Second, the book of Genesis describes how Jacob found his beloved at that well. In a similar but much more profound way, Jesus intends to prepare for a marriage. This latter marriage, though, will be a divine coupling far exceeding anyone's natural expectations.

Next, we read that Jesus sits down beside the well because he is wearied with his journey (Jn 4:6). This doesn't seem that important to our modern minds. Of course Jesus is tired from walking, and of course he sits down to take a breather. That sounds normal. Yet many commentators remark that Jesus' weariness is on a theological and pastoral level more than on a physical plane. He is wearied by human sin, which puts a great distance between human beings and God. He has traversed that great divide by becoming fully human, and though he is without sin, he has embraced our humanity in all its ugliness. He is weary, and he will continue to work tirelessly to bring us to conversion.

The last detail that John provides to set the scene is to tell us what time of day it is. "It was about the sixth hour," he writes (Jn 4:6). In biblical parlance, "the sixth hour" refers to the sixth hour after sunrise. Given that the sun rises at roughly 6:00 a.m. in that part of the world, "the sixth hour" refers to the noonday hour, the time when the sun is directly overhead and there are no shadows. Thus, "the sixth hour" represents the time of the greatest light. In John's Gospel account, the contrast between dark, representing sin and the reign of the enemy, and light, representing God's life, love, and grace, is on nearly every page. Here John clearly means to signify that God's very life and grace are present in this moment and in this location.

The woman who thirsts

Now that the scene is set with those small but crucial details, the encounter can begin. "There came a woman of Samaria to draw water" (Jn 4:7). Note that this woman is coming to draw water at noon. All the other women of the town would have come early in the day to avoid the brutal sunlight and heat of the desert. Given the culture of that day and place, either the woman must be trying to avoid other women, or she is shunned by them, or both.

It is also important to note that Jesus seeks out a woman. Throughout his public ministry, the Messiah continually approaches and makes significant revelations to women. This reveals two important facts. First, women are equal to men in their potential for conversion and discipleship in the Christian life. This is something radically new that Christianity brings to the

world, as other philosophies and religions subordinate the contri-
bution of the female sex. Second, on a theological level, we might
glean that all discipleship happens in a female mode, a mode of
receptivity. God is the divine giver, and all disciples are receivers,
just as females are naturally receivers. So, in the life of conversion,
this woman stands for all of us, and we must learn to be more like
her. Augustine teaches that we disciples ought to see ourselves in
the Samaritan woman "and in her give thanks to God" for the
conversion that he has wrought in us.[13]

The first words of this divine encounter remind us again of
the primacy of grace, that God always moves first. "Give me a
drink," Jesus says to the Samaritan woman (Jn 4:7). These words
first express the Lord's thirst, his desire for a holy relationship
with this woman, and for her response in faith. This is the same
thirst that he has for every one of us; it is the same thirst that
he will express on the cross (Jn 19:28). As disciples, we do well
to remember that every movement of our mouths, minds, and
hearts is only in response to the God who is already moving to
bring us nearer to him, the God who deeply desires to be in full
relationship with us.

The woman does not expect this approach from Jesus, and
her indignant response shows her surprise. "How is it that you,
a Jew, ask a drink of me, a woman of Samaria?" she asks (Jn
4:9). There are several things revealed in her response. First there
is the cultural dissonance between Jews and Samaritans. In this
woman's world, no Jew would want anything from one whom
he views as dirty or less than religiously upright. Next there is
the social impropriety of a man speaking to a woman in public.
Finally there is her deep sinfulness, which has caused her social
isolation. This woman probably believes that she is unlovable and
that no decent man could desire anything pure from her. This
woman is ready to cling to the well-established mores that domi-
nate first-century Palestinian culture. At least in word, she wants

to remain in her comfort zone.

As disciples in the lifelong process of conversion, we must come to expect the unexpected, because God will surprise us in his work of drawing near to us. He will overcome anything that prevents relationship with him, including social customs. And at the same time, he will obliterate our comfort zones.

The gift of grace

Jesus' next comment returns us to the theme of God's abundant grace. "If you knew the *gift of God*," the Lord replies, "and who it is that is saying to you, 'Give me a drink,' you would have asked him and he would have given you *living water*" (Jn 4:10; emphasis added). With these two key phrases, we are inside what Bishop Robert Barron calls "the circle of grace."[14] The gift of God is his "free and undeserved help" to allow us to come into, or back into, right relationship with him. Moreover, water always has been a substantial sign of God's life and his covenantal love for his chosen people. In the New Testament, John tells us, this relationship will take on new, dynamic qualities. It will bring new life!

These early moments of the conversation begin to make the woman aware of her desire and her need for grace. In a very particular way, the "living water" that Jesus offers is in stark contrast with the natural water that this woman has come to draw from this well. Jesus tells the woman, "Every one who drinks of this water will thirst again, but whoever drinks of the water that I shall give him will never thirst; the water that I shall give him will become in him a spring of water welling up to eternal life" (Jn 4:13–14).

This statement is pivotal in bringing her to a deeper realization that she cannot provide for herself what she seeks. This "living water," of which God is the only source, will provide infinite supernatural sustenance. Indeed, he is *the* infinite and supernatural! Here, the Word of God speaks directly to her heart about the deepest longing of the human heart, about the purpose for which she has been created. The Lord lets her know that perfect fulfillment is possible. The fact that he offers himself to us in the life of discipleship is sheer gift, sheer grace.

Her answer is like the moment when the prodigal son comes to his senses, and it is also a cry of repentance. She is now taking the first steps in the life of conversion and discipleship. "Sir," she cries, "give me this water, that I may not thirst, nor come here to draw" (Jn 4:15). On the surface, we know that she wants to avoid coming to the well because she is a social outcast. However, there is a deeper, spiritual meaning of her words. She is coming to realize that the living water offered by Jesus will quench her spiritual thirst. She will no longer have to search for deeper meaning and fulfillment in natural places, or be bound by cultural customs that force her to avoid people because she is living in sin. The living water will transcend that, and she cries out for it. She desires the freedom she senses can be found in the water this mysterious man can provide for her.

The moments that I cried out to the Lord for living water, for something that would rescue me from my misery, are vivid in my memory. When I entered college, I immediately took up fraternity life, and did so with an unhealthy and unholy zeal. After a while, I became disillusioned with that lifestyle, and I even began to perceive that my relationships were not going to lift me up and bring me to fulfillment. I would sit on my bed without moving, or I would stare out the window of my house, or I would drive around for long periods of time. I longed for meaning in my life and deeper fulfillment.

Jesus was probably very weary of the condition I was in. Yet he found me to be worth the effort. He began to break into my existential crisis, and bit by bit, he offered to me the same living water that he offered to the Samaritan woman. Following my response to his initial offer, Jesus has continued to provide that living water for sustenance all along my journey with him.

He will do the same for anyone and everyone who comes to the font of his grace, no matter how many times we present ourselves as weary and worn outcasts. One of the key components of a life of ongoing conversion is to recognize our weariness and to return to that well. In meeting Jesus there, time after time, we will become more certain that he is the only one who can provide the spiritual sustenance, the grace, that we need.

Deeper conversion, greater freedom

With her request for living water, the woman has expressed an initial desire for conversion. But conversion doesn't happen only once, and it doesn't remain on a surface level. She must be moved to a deeper, total transformation and purification. Indeed, she is coming to understand and believe that this is possible. Not only does she believe that it is possible, but she also comes to desire that transformation and purification. She comes to desire the new life of freedom that she senses is possible with this man before her.

This process of transformation begins in the next segment of their conversation. Jesus instructs her, "Go, call your husband, and come here" (Jn 4:16). The woman's admission that she has no husband allows the Lord to enter into this broken and wounded area of her life. Gently, Jesus tells her that "you have had five husbands, and he whom you now have is not your husband" (Jn 4:17–18). This is clearly a deep source of pain for this woman. Not only is it the reason she has been ostracized from Samaritan social circles, but she must feel that she is a failure as a person.

Augustine also provides a spiritual sense of the woman's situation. He explains that her five husbands provide an analogy to the five human senses and the five books of the Torah. In the first case, Augustine teaches us that this woman has attempted to find fulfillment in base sensuality. In the second, she has formed a misguided understanding and application of God's law, forming her religion around her own thoughts and preferences.[15] Clearly, everything she has sought to this point in her life has been insufficient. She has not found what, or the One, she seeks. It is a significant moment of conversion when growing disciples realize that nothing else is enough to satisfy their desires. In the words of Saint Teresa of Avila, "God alone is enough." Yet because of our prideful and sinful ways, we are probably going to have this realization many times throughout our discipleship journey.

The significance of this moment does not end there. Jesus tells the woman that she has had five husbands, and there is a man in her life now who is not her husband (Jn 4:18). That makes six men. Now, Jesus stands before her as the seventh man in her life. Seven is the biblical number of wholeness, God's perfect number. Here, in the person of Jesus Christ, God offers a holy, fulfilling relationship that will bring healing, joy, and (as we will see) courage. This is true for all of us, not just the Samaritan woman. The Lord wants to provide us with that same healing, joy, and freedom — that living water that she receives by the well.

The conversation then moves to the topic of religion and right worship. This exchange allows Jesus to lead the Samaritan woman from her perception that he is a prophet (Jn 4:19), a religious sage of some kind, to the revelation that he is the Messiah whom the Jews and, to an extent, the Samaritans await. The best part of this episode is the moment when Jesus reveals his true identity (Jn 4:26). He uses the same statement that God once made to Moses in revealing his name: "I AM" (Ex 3:14).[16] Jesus is conveying to this woman that right worship will not be determined by its geographic location, but by its orientation to God, who is spirit and truth (Jn 4:21–24. This is her opportunity to turn from a misguided understanding of religion to a full and life-giving relationship with the Lord.

It is our opportunity as well. Every one of us must have a moment (or many moments) of encounter when we come to know that Jesus is God, and that God calls us beyond what we have previously known. This encounter will not only lead us beyond our comfort zones but also toward "the glorious liberty of the children of God" about which Saint Paul writes in that powerful passage of Romans (8:21). The episode at the well in Samaria leads the woman to such liberty.

Leaving the old way behind

When Jesus' disciples return from procuring provisions, the biblical text tells us something extraordinarily powerful. "So the woman left her water jar, and went away into the city, and said to the people, 'Come, see a man who told me all that I ever did. Can this be the Christ?'" (Jn 4:28–29). There are several important layers here to unpack.

First, she leaves her water jar. Remember, she lives in the desert. Not only that, but she has become a social outcast, and this jar is likely one of her only possessions that provides sustenance and comfort. Yet the encounter she has just had with Jesus causes her to choose to leave her comforting possessions. How different this is from the young man we discussed in chapter 1. This woman has few possessions, and still she makes a choice for Christ. She has been gifted the freedom to choose him over everything else.

She doesn't just leave her water jar and return to her old way of life. Instead, she "went away into the city," Sychar, the very city where she is a social pariah because of her immoral lifestyle. And she doesn't just go into the city to have a latte and go shopping. She goes to the very people who have cast her out, and she begins to tell them of her encounter with Jesus. She has become the very first proclaimer of the Good News in all the Gospels.

Augustine provides us with a powerful reflection about the woman's credibility to preach. He writes that "having received Christ the Lord into her heart, what could she do now but leave her water jar and run to preach the gospel? She cast out lust and hurried to proclaim the truth. Let those who would preach the gospel learn: let them throw away their water jar at the well." The woman is so eager to be satisfied by the living water that her jar becomes burdensome, Augustine tells us.[17]

Let's also focus for just a moment on the woman's confession. She tells her fellow citizens that this man "told me all that I ever did." She only knows that Jesus has told her this much because she has been able to examine her conscience and become aware of the ways that she has acted outside of God's plan. She might not tell each and every citizen each and every immoral act that she has committed, but she knows enough to declare that once her life was one way, and now she can live in a very different way. Our encounters with Jesus provide each of us with the freedom to admit that we have done wrong, that we have not lived according to his plan for our lives. Even those of us who have been walking as committed disciples for years must admit this frequently. Until we reach the moment of death and judgment, we are always in a process of conversion.

The conversion of a town

Soon after this, John's Gospel tells us, "Many Samaritans from that city believed in [Jesus] because of the woman's testimony" (4:39). Did you catch that? They believe in Jesus as Messiah, based simply on this woman's encounter with him. This is the power of letting our conversions be known. People will recognize that we are different, and we will be able to tell them it is because we have met Jesus Christ and he has changed us.

So these citizens come out to meet Jesus, and then they ask him to stay with them. He obliges and remains two more days with them (Jn 4:40). Surely, during these two days, the Lord prays with them and teaches them about the fullness of God's plan, which they don't fully understand because they are not part of God's covenant people. Their own encounter with Jesus has a transformative effect on them. "And many more believed because of his word," the Gospel text tells us (Jn 4:41). Indeed, something powerful has happened: "They said to the woman, 'It is no longer because of your words that we believe, for we have heard for ourselves, and we know that this is indeed the Savior of the world'" (Jn 4:42).

This outcast woman has been given an amazing freedom by her encounter with Jesus, and she has shared it with others, inviting them to come and encounter him also. Once they decide to meet Jesus, they have their own encounter with him, and they believe based on that, not on someone else's testimony. That's the way evangelization and conversion work: I tell someone of my experience and invite them to come and meet the Lord. After that person meets Jesus, they no longer rely on my experience of freedom. That person has his or her own experience of freedom in Christ.

This episode in John's Gospel is one of the best examples in Scripture of a person finding and experiencing the freedom that God provides. This is a story that any of us can return to again and again, to find for ourselves the healing, the hope, and the freedom that we all seek. Perhaps it will also give us the courage and zeal to go to others and share the ways that the Lord has transformed us, so that they might be transformed as well.

QUESTIONS FOR DEEPER
UNDERSTANDING AND REFLECTION

1. Can you recall a divine appointment in your own life, something that was unexpected in your plan but arranged by the Lord so something beautiful could happen?

2. What do you have to offer to Jesus that will quench his thirst?

3. Can you describe a moment when you cried out for the living water that God offers?

4. Have you ever been excited and encouraged enough to leave worldly comforts behind for the sake of sharing the Good News? Have you had the opportunity to share your encounter with Jesus with others? What happened?

Chapter 6

DISCIPLESHIP

Prayerfully read Mark 10:46–52

Discipleship has been a hot topic, even a buzzword, in the Catholic Church in the United States in recent years. Sherry Weddell's popular book *Forming Intentional Disciples* argues effectively that there is a journey of conversion that leads to intentional discipleship. In his first apostolic exhortation, *Evangelii Gaudium* (The Joy of the Gospel), Pope Francis urges us to become a Church of missionary disciples (119–121). Parishes and dioceses all over the country are placing new emphasis on this, which is a positive sign, a trend in the right direction. After all, one of the two commandments that Jesus gives to his Church is to "Go therefore and make disciples" (Mt 28:18).[18]

Of course, there are many episodes in the Gospels that illuminate the path of discipleship that the Lord wants us to take. We have already dealt with some of them. But I think there is one short episode that illustrates, better than any other, that discipleship is the end point of the conversion process. It is the story of Bartimaeus, the blind beggar outside of Jericho. This episode reveals important dimensions about how total and complete conversion can and should be in our lives.[19]

Blindness

The first detail we read is that "they came to Jericho" (Mk 10:46). The importance of this fact will be lost on us unless we know a little bit about ancient geography and culture. Recall when Jericho is first mentioned in the Bible: It is the city that the Israelites must conquer first as they enter the promised land after wandering in the desert for forty years. The city is full of people who don't know, and live contrary to, God's plan. It is a wicked city. This understanding of Jericho prevails throughout the rest of the Bible, and any time Jericho is mentioned, it carries this meaning. Jericho stands for the sinfulness of the world. So this episode in

Mark's Gospel provides a stark image of the battle between Jesus and sin. It is a new conquering of the ancient "sin city." Only this time, it is a spiritual conquering, because Jesus calls a man to conversion. This is far weightier than the previous military conquering, and it extends into our own lives as well. Jesus has come into our world and our lives to conquer sin.

Outside of Jericho, we meet Bartimaeus. He is the "son of Timaeus," "a blind beggar," and he is "sitting by the roadside" (Mk 10:46). First, it is interesting that the author mentions Bartimaeus's family lineage. The Gospel writers rarely name the parents of people whom Jesus heals. Based on this fact, Augustine asserts that "there can be little doubt that this Bartimaeus, the son of Timaeus, had fallen from some position of great prosperity, and was now regarded as an object of the most notorious and the most remarkable wretchedness."[20]

The description of Bartimaeus also notes that he is blind. Blindness was a serious issue in the Jewish culture of Jesus' day, and it has been so throughout the history of God's people. There are several passages in the Old Testament that speak of physical and spiritual blindness (see the books of Lamentations and Isaiah, for example). In the Bible, blindness symbolizes sin, living contrary to God's plan. Elsewhere in the Gospels, we learn that many people in Jesus' day assumed that blindness (or any infirmity) was a punishment for sin, even the sins of one's parents. Consider the scene in John 9, when Jesus and his disciples happen upon a man born blind. The disciples ask, "Rabbi, who sinned, this man or his parents, that he was born blind?" (Jn 9:2). Jesus replies that the man's blindness is not due to his or his parents' sins, but exists so that "the works of God might be made manifest in him" (Jn 9:3). The same is true of Bartimaeus: Jesus has come to call him to a life of discipleship so that he might participate in the works of God.

The ultimate point here is that we must allow Jesus to heal

our spiritual blindness. Each of us has this blindness because we are born with original sin, we suffer its effects, and we live in a world wracked by sin.

Moreover, Mark tells us that Bartimaeus is "sitting by the roadside." This simple detail emphasizes his outcast and down-trodden social position and underscores the other parts of the description. There would have been many people walking to Jerusalem, preparing for the Passover feast. But not this blind beggar. He is disabled and isolated.[21] Like the Samaritan woman at the well, he has been cast out of the higher social circles as one who is not useful.

Calling out to Jesus

When Bartimaeus learns that "it was Jesus" passing by, he reacts in a surprising way. We read that "he began to cry out," yelling, "Jesus, Son of David, have mercy on me!" (Mk 10:47). There is much richness in this short statement.

First, there is the name of Jesus, which Bartimaeus shouts. It is interesting that Bartimaeus is the only person healed by Jesus in Mark's Gospel account who calls the Lord by that name. Others call him Messiah, Rabbi, or Lord. Yet Bartimaeus provides Christians with a very powerful example. Christians are taught that the name of Jesus is our very salvation. The Acts of the Apostles tells us that "there is no other name under heaven given among men by which we must be saved" (4:12). The *Catechism of the Catholic Church* states it more simply: "Jesus means … 'God saves'" (430). Later, the *Catechism* states this even more powerfully: Jesus is the "one name that contains everything," and it is the name that contains the "whole economy of creation and salvation. To pray 'Jesus' is to invoke him and to call him within us" (2666). Even in our own lives, calling on the name of Jesus has a special resonance and power. His name should be frequently on our lips!

Next, Bartimaeus connects himself and Jesus to the rich history of Israel by calling Jesus "Son of David." In Jesus' day, all of Israel was awaiting a descendant of the greatest king the nation had ever known. Israel knew their salvation would come through a Davidic heir, a messiah who would "restore the Davidic monarchy and rule over Israel forever."[22] This is why Matthew and Luke spend so much ink and effort in their Gospel accounts to illustrate that Jesus is descended from David on both Joseph's and Mary's side of his lineage. Bartimaeus, even if he is not a Jew, knows enough Jewish history and culture to hedge his bets that this man can do something powerful for him.

Bartimaeus's next words are perhaps the most powerful of the whole episode. He cries out to Jesus: "Have mercy on me" (Mk 10:47). Having only heard about this Jesus of Nazareth, Bartimaeus knows what the Messiah's mission is. Jesus has come to our world, taken on our humanity, precisely to have mercy upon us. Saint Thomas Aquinas, quoting Augustine, defines mercy well: Mercy is "heartfelt sympathy for another's distress." This is why, both Augustine and Aquinas remind us, the Latin word for mercy is *misericordia*, "denoting a man's compassionate heart (*miserum cor*) for another's unhappiness."[23] Bartimaeus is begging Jesus to minister compassionately to his distress and unhappiness.

It is also important for us to realize that each one of us enters into this moment in our Catholic liturgy. In the penitential rite at Mass, we cry out, "*Kyrie, eleison*" (or its English translation, "Lord, have mercy"). The Greek verb here is *eleeó*, which means "to have pity or mercy on, to show mercy." More specifically, it invokes God's covenant mercy, the same mercy that he has shown throughout salvation history to the Israelites and wayward tribes.

I frequently need Jesus to minister to my distress and unhappiness, and to have mercy on me. I recall hearing this Gospel reading at Mass one Sunday and then thinking for the whole following week, "I am nothing other than a beggar upon the Lord's mercy." Whether I am distressed about something at work, or unhappy about family relationships, I need to ask Jesus to minister to that. The problem is remembering to ask him to come into those situations. To become better at remembering, I have recently begun employing the "Jesus Prayer," which has been a staple of eastern Christian spirituality for centuries and which resembles Bartimaeus's words in this Gospel passage. The prayer goes, "Lord Jesus Christ, Son of God, have mercy on me, a sinner."[24] It adds only a few words to Bartimaeus's cry. I have found this prayer helpful and fruitful in my own prayer life. Every time I have a few extra moments, I breathe in, saying "Lord, Jesus Christ, son of God," and then I breathe out, saying, "have mercy on me, a sinner." I find that it affects my whole attitude and day, centering me again in my walk with the Lord and my dealings with others. It also reminds me that I am still a sinner in need of conversion and God's grace and mercy.

Many in the crowd rebuke Bartimaeus, telling him to be quiet. Essentially, they are telling him not to bother this important figure, Jesus. Or perhaps they are trying to ensure that they get to make their own requests of Jesus. This raises some important questions, which each of us should apply to our own life. Ask yourself: Have I ever been kept quiet by others as I have called out to Jesus? Have I allowed my pleas to the Lord to be silenced or impacted by what others think or say? Perhaps more poignantly, have I ever tried to keep someone else quiet as he or she called out to Jesus? These types of questions are vital in our spiritual lives, our lives of conversion. Do we let others keep us from encountering Jesus and turning more fully toward him, perhaps because we don't want to "rock the boat" or "make a scene"? Have we kept others from an encounter with Jesus for the same or similar reasons?

Thankfully, Bartimaeus does not give up his search for the Lord's mercy. Instead, "he cried out all the more, 'Son of David, have mercy on me'" (Mk 10:48). Bartimaeus's deep cry is effective. The next three words might be some of the most striking in all the Gospels: "And Jesus stopped" (Mk 10:49). Because Bartimaeus will not let his search for mercy be thwarted, he causes Jesus to stop in his tracks, to halt momentarily his progress from Jericho to Jerusalem. This should remind each of us that we cannot let our quest for the Lord be squelched. When we encounter difficulties, even from other people, we must cry out to God all the more loudly and frequently. Sometimes God is simply waiting for us to express how much we want to be in relationship with him before he answers.

Called by Jesus

Then Jesus speaks two powerful words: "Call him." Every time I read these words I am reminded that every person ever created has a vocation, a call that has been given by God. First, each of us is called to holiness. Then, each of us also has a calling to a particular state in life. In my case, I have been called to married life, to be a good and holy husband, and to bring children into this world and raise them for the glory of the kingdom. Next, each person has a unique calling addressed to him or her alone. I have been called to minister to the people of the parish community where God has placed me. I also feel called to write for God's glory. In each area of our vocation, we are all far from perfect and very much in need of conversion. Each day, our prayer should be for God's grace to help us become better, more in tune with, and more open to his will.

So, Bartimaeus is called before Jesus. The Bible tells us that "they called the blind man, saying to him, 'Take heart; rise, he is calling you'" (Mk 10:49). I have often wondered who "they" are. Is it the people in the crowd? Only a moment before, they were shushing the blind man; now they are encouraging him to go quickly to the Messiah. Perhaps the crowd is not seriously seeking Jesus' mercy and a relationship with him. Like many of the crowds that follow Jesus, they may simply want to see some miracle or other and then go on their way. And Jesus calls Bartimaeus instead of anyone else in the crowd. In his divine wisdom, he knows who among them is experiencing conversion of heart and seeking relationship with him.

But perhaps it isn't the crowd but the disciples who tell Bartimaeus to "take heart." In my opinion, this makes more sense. Why? Because the disciples have already been the recipients of Jesus' powerful and encouraging words. There is one other place in the Gospels where the phrase "Take heart" is used. It is when the disciples are "terrified" to see Jesus walking on the Sea of Galilee, thinking he is a ghost. In that moment, Jesus says to them, "Take heart, it is I; have no fear" (Mt 14:26–27). In that case, Jesus invites his disciples to a deeper trust. Now that they have experienced the encouragement of the Lord, they can give it to others. Conversion of heart and life enables us to encourage others to walk the same path that we walk.

Bartimaeus's response is nothing short of inspiring. "And throwing off his cloak he sprang up and came to Jesus" (Mk 10:50). He is not afraid, nor is he attached to his possessions. We have already seen that both these attitudes are necessary for entering into a deep, fulfilling relationship with Jesus. Perhaps the cloak is symbolic of the sinful life Bartimaeus previously lived. Now, when he meets Jesus, he casts it aside because he has found what he ultimately wants.

I have experienced this too. When I found Jesus, encountered his mercy, and was offered a deep and satisfying relationship with him, I cast off my previous life of being focused solely on sensual pleasures and self-aggrandizement. At least I started to cast it off. My conversion remains an ongoing process. Day by day I try to submit to God's grace, which will help me grow in the virtues I so desperately need: humility, gratitude, generosity, temperance, and charity chief among them. Throwing off the cloak of vice takes time, but it makes my life much better than it was previously. I am freer now than I ever have been.

"Let me receive my sight"

When Bartimaeus comes before Jesus, the Lord asks him a powerful question: "What do you want me to do for you?" Bartimaeus responds, "Master, let me receive my sight" (Mk 10:51). Sight is one of the five senses. Without it, we cannot know the world or ourselves fully. Without sight, we can easily be taken advantage of. Clearly, in the physical and social sense, the blind man wants to be healed.

However, the Fathers of the Church and Scripture scholars down through the ages have read this as a request not only for physical sight. They believe that Bartimaeus asks for spiritual sight as well. Isn't that what Jesus has come to provide, in ancient Israel and in our lives? We would all do well to ask Jesus to remove our spiritual blindness and let us see truth, goodness, and beauty so that we can live life well.

Try this exercise. Put yourself in Bartimaeus's place and imagine the Lord asking you that question.

How would you respond?

Our answer to this question reveals the deepest desires of our hearts. Perhaps you want a healed and holy marriage. Perhaps you want a return to faith or other good things for your children. Perhaps you want success in your work, whether it be secular or Church-related. Underneath all these desires, however, there must be a deeper and more lasting desire: the desire to relate more fully to the Holy Trinity and to lead a holy life pleasing to God. This is the spiritual sight that we need; we need to recognize what our desires truly are and what they should be. Of course we need to be converted from our former blindness. But we also need to be converted from our focus on things that are in themselves good but less important than living according to God's design for our lives.

Jesus responds in the affirmative to Bartimaeus's desire. The Lord tells the blind man that his faith has made him well (Mk 10:52). It is interesting that the Greek word (*sōzō*) translated here as "made you well" can also be translated as "saved you." So we see that there are multiple dimensions to this request and this miracle. Bartimaeus is now able to see not only with his eyes but also with his heart, more clearly than he ever has. The next sentence confirms this. The Gospel writer tells us, "And immediately he received his sight" (Mk 10:52).

"Go your way"

Before Jesus tells Bartimaeus that he will be healed, he tells him, "Go *your* way" (Mk 10:52, emphasis added). Jesus tells Bartimaeus that he is free to go about his life as he freely chooses, even if it means that Bartimaeus will not follow him. Yet after receiving his sight, the healed man chooses freely: Bartimaeus "followed him on *the way*" (Mk 10:52, emphasis added). In this episode, "the way" is far different from "your way." "Your way" refers to a person's freedom to go about his own business. "The way" means following Jesus as a disciple. It is no coincidence that early Christianity was called "the Way."[25] Jesus gives Bartimaeus freedom to walk away, to go about his own worldly business. Yet, with the new spiritual sight that he has received from the Lord, Bartimaeus chooses to become a Christian disciple, because he can see with his heart that it will be more satisfying than the way he has been living up to this point.

I find Bartimaeus's decision to be greatly inspiring, a model for all disciples. The process of conversion is about having "Bartimaeus moments" again and again in our walk with the Lord. We should continually be asking Jesus to open the eyes of our hearts.

It is worth noting here that many Scripture scholars, including some Church Fathers, see this story of Bartimaeus as an allegory for the Gentile nations. The nations that have not known the one true God are spiritually blind. Jesus coming to them (by visiting places like Samaria and Jericho) and calling them allows them to see the full truth that God reveals and to find the salvation they wouldn't otherwise have. This can provide great inspiration for our evangelization efforts in the modern world. We must take Jesus to the modern-day "Jerichos," whatever those might be, asking God to grant them deeper spiritual insight too.

Finally, note that Jericho, according to Mark's Gospel, is Jesus' last stop before entering Jerusalem. Jesus is going to his death, and his disciples are called to follow him. But we do so remembering that the Resurrection follows the crucifixion, the city of glory follows immediately after the city of sin. Jesus heals and teaches on his way to Jerusalem, where he will complete the ultimate act of healing: providing the redemption about which he has been teaching. For Bartimaeus and for all of us as disciples, following Jesus means going with him all the way to the cross (Lk 9:23).

QUESTIONS FOR DEEPER
UNDERSTANDING AND REFLECTION

1. Are there areas in your life where the Lord has shown you your spiritual blindness? How did he reveal this to you?

2. Do you think it is important to say the name "Jesus" frequently? What are some things you can do to make this a habit in your life, if it is not already?

3. What is the unique calling the Lord has given to you? Can you describe the various layers of your vocation?

4. Can you describe a moment when you asked Jesus for spiritual sight you didn't have before? What happened?

5. What does it mean for you to follow Jesus on the Way? How has growing in discipleship impacted your life?

Chapter 7

MISSION AND THE WORKS OF MERCY

Prayerfully read Luke 19:1–10

In the Gospel of Luke, we encounter a person who is able to draw near to the Lord despite being perceived as far from the heart of God. Luke tells the story of a conversion that is unexpected yet total. It is the story of Zacchaeus, the "wee little man" about whom many of us sang as children. The story of Zacchaeus's conversion inspires and impels us to engage in mission and the works of mercy. His story reminds us that once we have encountered Jesus, our life naturally becomes about lifting up others.

Hindrances to God's plan

This story also takes place at Jericho, this time inside the city. Here we meet "a man named Zacchaeus," and we learn two details about him: He is "a chief tax collector" and he is "rich." Now, to our modern sensibilities, these two details might not mean much. He has a job and a little bit of wealth. How is this problematic? However, this is not how Luke's audience would have received these details. To be a tax collector was to be perceived as a swindler, because tax collectors skimmed money off the top of their collections. In fact, they added money to the amounts that the Roman government expected them to collect so they could keep more for themselves. That's how they made their living. Not only that, but tax collectors worked for Rome, and loyal Jews didn't much care for Roman authority. Therefore, tax collectors were viewed as disloyal to the Jewish nation — and this was just how they felt about regular tax collectors. Zacchaeus was a chief tax collector and would have been viewed as the most depraved of all of them. Faithful Jews would have wanted to cast him away from the community for violating the covenant.

Moreover, Zacchaeus was not a poor tax collector. He was wealthy. In Jewish spirituality, wealth could be an obstacle to drawing near to God and finding the Lord's favor, if a person trusted in wealth more than in God. Think of the rich young man we studied near the beginning of this book. For Zacchaeus to be described as rich might have been used as a literary device to illustrate that he was far from God's heart and far from the covenant people. So Zacchaeus is perceived as facing two difficult obstacles to encountering God and living in the divine life and love.

Finding Jesus by any means necessary

Despite these obstacles, Luke tells us that Zacchaeus "sought to see who Jesus was" (Lk 19:3). In this ancient culture, a wealthy tax collector in Jericho likely would not have wanted to see Jesus or relate to God on a deep level. Yet Zacchaeus does. This is the first and most important moment of his conversion to Jesus. The desire to convert and enter into relationship with the Lord is the most important detail of conversion. The Lord always answers in the affirmative if the desire is present in a person.

This still applies to us in the Church today. There are many people in our world who are seeking Jesus, even if they are far from him at their starting point. Indeed, they may have a long way to go, just as many of us have been far from God at different points in our lives. Yet God's grace can make up for infinite chasms. We must never limit what we think God can do; he can bring anyone, even the most hardened sinner, into the life of grace in the way that most pleases and glorifies him.

Still, despite his good desires, Zacchaeus has a problem. He cannot see Jesus "on account of the crowd, because he was small of stature" (Lk 19:3). There were large crowds of people trying to catch a glimpse of this miracle-working Messiah, and Zacchaeus was shorter than the average Jew of his day. Yet there is a deeper significance to these statements in the allegorical meaning of the words of the Bible. These words tell us about Zacchaeus's character. Commenting on this passage, Saint Cyril of Alexandria writes, "Zacchaeus searched to see Christ, but the multitude prevented him, not so much that of the people but of his sins. He was short of stature, not merely in a bodily point of view but also spiritually. He could not see him unless he were raised up from the earth."[26] Isn't this exactly the type of person to whom Jesus has ministered throughout the Gospels? Those racked with sin, those cast out from mainstream society? This is precisely when and where the most profound conversions happen, not only in Jesus' public ministry, but also in our own day. We are lifted up by God's grace, we are most ripe for conversion, when we are spiritually small and unable to help ourselves.

Next, we read that Zacchaeus "ran on ahead and climbed up into a sycamore tree" because Jesus was about to pass that way (Lk 19:4). Most of us in a similar situation would probably immediately wonder how this might look to the crowd. Since the earliest days of Christianity, however, it has been taught that it is better to be a fool for Christ (1 Cor 4:10) than wise in the ways of men because "the foolishness of God is wiser than men" (1 Cor 1:25). Laying down our egos and our social standing may be difficult, but it is exactly what we need to do in order to allow Jesus to come to us just as he came to this tax collector.

It is also interesting that Zacchaeus runs to where he knows Jesus will be, so that he can climb the tree and catch a glimpse of this Messiah. Because he knows where Jesus will be, he is able to calculate the best way to see him, and perhaps to speak with him. For those of us who have already embarked on a life of conversion, we need to follow Zacchaeus's example here. We need to run to the place where we know Jesus will be, so we can see him and talk to him. This might be in Eucharistic adoration, or before the tabernacle in a quiet church, where Jesus is truly present in the Eucharist, waiting for us.

The invitation and the gaze

While Zacchaeus is in the tree, Jesus arrives at the location. He notices the man in the tree. This makes sense, after all: Most of us would notice that there is a man in a tree when no other members of the crowd are in trees. Yet, in his divinity, Jesus can sense this man's desire to encounter what is true, good, and beautiful. So Jesus goes to the tree and looks up at Zacchaeus (Lk 19:5). This is a small but profoundly striking detail. Jesus here looks up at a person on whom a whole culture looks down. This is a great example of Jesus' humility, which lifts us up from our lowly position. It is a beautiful (and humbling) exercise for us to ponder the reason(s) that Jesus must "look up" to us. Perhaps it is our kindness or hospitality. Perhaps it is our depth of knowledge about particular subjects. Perhaps it is our deep desire to intercede for others in prayer. Whatever it is, we should feel in this gaze of Jesus the same love with which Jesus looked upon the young man with great possessions who went away sad. This is the same love with which Jesus looks at Zacchaeus. Like Zacchaeus, we can choose to respond with joy. The difference is that we can be transformed by Jesus' gaze if we are ready and open.

Jesus then invites the tax collector into a relationship. "Zacchaeus, make haste and come down; for I must stay at your house today" (Lk 19:5). The first thing that should strike us is the phrase "make haste." There are two other key moments in the Gospels when a person or a group does something with "haste." The first is when Mary visits Elizabeth in the hill country of Judea, immediately after the Annunciation of the Messiah's birth. The second is when the shepherds in the fields go with haste to Bethlehem to see the newborn Savior. All three of these instances of "haste" happen to be recorded in Luke's Gospel. I think he is trying to illustrate that we "make haste" when we are ready for a transformative encounter with Christ, or when we are excited to help someone else have that encounter. In the case of Zacchaeus, because his heart has been turned toward the Lord he, can move with haste away from his previous way of life.

Jesus tells Zacchaeus that he must stay at his house that very day. Augustine provides a powerful reflection on this line. "Christ," the saint writes, "who was already dwelling in his heart, is welcomed into his house."[27] Zacchaeus's "house," in this instance his physical dwelling, is analogous to his soul. Jesus wants to take up permanent residence in the heart of this man who is already disposed to welcome him fully. The question for us today is clear: Is Jesus already dwelling fully in our hearts? If not, are we ready for him to move in?

Zacchaeus is ready. Luke tells us, "So he made haste and came down, and received him joyfully" (Lk 19:6). Zacchaeus responds exactly to Jesus' command: He makes haste. The tax collector is ready to encounter Jesus. His desire is met so perfectly that he becomes full of joy. There can be no other emotional response from a disciple, even a brand-new disciple, other than joy. Joy is the quintessential marker of a transformative encounter with the Lord.

I recall this being the case during the summer after I was received into the Catholic Church. I just had to tell people that I had become Catholic, whether they cared or not! I remember going on a vehicle test-drive and telling the car salesman that I had become Catholic. I also remember one instance when I was working an internship at a local museum system and telling one of the museum curators how excited I was. I don't think she was interested in religion, but she sure knew that I was interested. That summer, I had a joy in my heart that has barely been matched since. It happens to all of us when we have a true, lasting encounter with Jesus.

The law of conversion and mercy

Sadly, there will always be those who are negative and even irritated by our joy. This was true for Zacchaeus as well. Luke tells us that the crowd murmurs in unison because Jesus "has gone in to be the guest of ... a sinner" (Lk 19:7). This crowd is clearly made up of Pharisees and their followers, because Pharisees would have been the leading critics of tax collectors. Pharisees saw themselves as the great protectors of the Jewish people, and tax collectors were grave sinners against the nation and the covenant. They would have told others that tax collectors were not only grave sinners, but also enemies of the people. Moreover, based on their conception of law and salvation, they would have said that there could be no redemption for someone in Zacchaeus's position. They could not fathom the law of conversion and mercy that Jesus Christ came to institute.

Yet Zacchaeus is not swayed by what the crowd thinks. His singular focus is a wonderful example for all of us. In any process of conversion, whether ancient or new, we must be guided by our desire for deeper relationship with Jesus. Nothing else can get in the way of that.

Zacchaeus will let nothing get in his way. He vows to Jesus, "Behold, Lord, the half of my goods I give to the poor; and if I have defrauded any one of anything, I restore it fourfold" (Lk 19:8). This is radical. The Mosaic law required only, at most, a twofold restitution.[28] Zacchaeus is doubling what is required by law, and he promises to give half of his possessions away to the poor. Saint Jerome, commenting on this passage, tells us that Zacchaeus "gave away his wealth and immediately replaced it with the riches of the heavenly kingdom."[29] Such a radical reaction is in line with the disposition of other characters that we've already studied, specifically the Samaritan woman and Bartimaeus. A real encounter with Jesus always leads us to make radical decisions and to begin to be radically generous.

This scene also indicates that Zacchaeus is promising to engage in the works of mercy. After all, if he is restoring money and giving goods to the poor, he will be feeding, clothing, and sheltering them, either directly or indirectly. Encountering Jesus does exactly this: It leads us to want to perform the works of mercy. We do this because we know, first, that every other person deserves to have such basic needs met because they too have been created in the image and likeness of God. Second, we know that performing works of mercy is exactly the way the Gospel is spread. Throughout the history of the Church, the most powerful tool for evangelization has been the works of mercy.

Jesus joyfully proclaims Zacchaeus's change of heart. "Today," the Lord tells Zacchaeus and the gathered crowd, "salvation has come to this house, since he also is a son of Abraham" (Lk 19:9). Zacchaeus enjoys equal footing with the rest of the crowd because of his religious heritage in Abraham, their father in faith. More than that, the Messiah proclaims that Zacchaeus can be, will be, a recipient of salvation because of these acts of great faith. Jesus wants the crowd to know that it is faith, and not works of the Mosaic law, that will bring them into right relationship with God and save them.

It is also important to realize that the works of mercy flow from faith in Jesus. Because of our relationship with him, and because of the salvation he offers, we can freely share that grace with others.

In the final verse of this passage, Jesus tells the crowd about his own mission: "For the Son of man came to seek and to save the lost" (Lk 19:10). In the case of Zacchaeus, Jesus has been seeking him all along. Even when Zacchaeus thought he was taking initiative by running and climbing a tree, the Holy Spirit had already moved in his heart, causing him to desire to meet Jesus. Once again, this is the principle of grace at work. God always moves first. Even our desire to seek him and relate to him is already a movement of his divine grace.

We cannot, however, leave everything to divine providence.

God expects that we will be active and that we will be agents of his plans. God has granted every human being the freedom to choose to come to the fullest expression of life. Not only can we choose that for ourselves, but we can also become like God by helping others to enter into a fuller life. That's why he has called us to engage in the works of mercy. This is precisely the way that he seeks and saves the lost in our world: by nudging us (slightly or not so slightly) to bring the Gospel to others by these amazing works, by helping others have a better life and experience the fullness of God's love.

QUESTIONS FOR DEEPER UNDERSTANDING AND REFLECTION

1. Who are the people in our own culture whom we assume to be far away from the Lord based on their careers or status? Why do we think this about them?

2. When did you come to know who Jesus is in a real and deep way? Did you do something radical to gain that understanding? How did God meet you in your search?

3. Has God ever prompted you to do something that seemed crazy so that you might have a deeper relationship with him?

4. Paragraph 2447 of the *Catechism of the Catholic Church* lists the spiritual and corporal works of mercy. Which works stand out to you most? Why? How can you engage in those works more fully?

Chapter 8

THE LIFE OF BEATITUDE

Prayerfully read Matthew 5:1–12

The conversion we have explored in this book brings us into the life of beatitude, which is enduring blessedness — or more simply, true happiness. The Beatitudes, spoken at the beginning of the Sermon on the Mount, are the quintessential expression of Christian discipleship. They represent the loftiest lifestyle for which a Christian can reach. None of us can claim to have experienced conversion in Jesus Christ — and to be living a true life of conversion — if we are not striving to live the life of beatitude presented here. Jesus is the perfect model of beatitude. Our minds and hearts and lives must be turned more fully to him each day if we want to live a true life of beatitude.

The crowds

Jesus has come not just for a few, but for many; and he has come to minister especially to the multitude of those who are on the fringes of ancient Palestinian and Jewish society. Note Matthew's use of the word "crowds" in the Sermon on the Mount (Mt 5:1). At the end of the previous chapter of Matthew's Gospel, we read that these crowds have begun following Jesus from every area of ancient Israel, including areas that weren't fully part of the Jewish religion, such as the Decapolis or the region "beyond the Jordan" (Mt 4:25). The Greek word is *ochlos*, which refers both to a multitude of people and to common people. Matthew here offers a significant insight into Jesus' ministry and mission.[30]

The Beatitudes, like all other passages and episodes in the Bible, are meant to apply to disciples in every era. Christ did not mean them simply as an antidote to the real and deep oppression in Israel's life at the time of his earthly ministry. They are the attitudes and actions that will alleviate the real and deep oppression that happens in our own age caused by sin and lack of trust in God's plan. In our own time, Catholics are reminded of this truth through Pope Francis's constant call for us to bring the Good News to people "on the fringes." The principle is the same: The Gospel of Jesus Christ is not intended for only a select few who have a certain social pedigree or financial means. We must allow God's grace to turn our hearts to this reality. We must be ready and willing to bring the Good News to the multitudes, to anyone who needs and wants to hear it.

Mountains and God's revelation

As Jesus prepares to teach about the Beatitudes, we read that "he went up on the mountain" (Mt 5:1). Matthew wants to depict Jesus as the new Moses, giving the new and perfect law from a mountain, just as the first prophet gave the old law from Mount Sinai. Moreover, in the Gospel accounts, there are relatively few instances of important events happening on or near mountains (especially in comparison with the Old Testament instances). We read that Jesus "went up into the hills by himself to pray" (Mt 14:23). There are the teachings about faith being able to move mountains. And in his Gospel Mark tells us that Jesus chose the Twelve Apostles on a mountain.

Other than those instances, there is only one other significant gospel event that takes place on a mountain: the Transfiguration. On Mount Tabor, we learn that Jesus is the fulfillment and perfection of the law (the Torah, represented by Moses) and the prophets (represented by Elijah, the first major prophet). We also learn that the only appropriate response to God's powerful and perfect revelation is to be "filled with awe" and to fall on our faces in worship like Peter, James, and John.

These two moments — Jesus' preaching about the Beatitudes and his Transfiguration on Mount Tabor — are intimately connected. The experience on Mount Tabor will be the fulfillment in act of what Jesus teaches on the Mount of the Beatitudes. When Jesus teaches his followers about the Beatitudes, he gives them the fulfillment of the Mosaic law. On Mount Tabor, the three apostles see and know that the Lord is the fulfillment of the law and the prophets, and they are instructed by the heavenly Father's voice to "listen to him" (Mt 17:5).

Looking at the Mount of the Beatitudes, let's examine this new law that Jesus presents as the perfect standard of discipleship. The first word that Jesus speaks reveals the underlying foundation and goal of this new law. The word is "blessed." This new law emanates from blessedness and leads us to blessedness. In the Greek texts, the word is *makarios*, which connotes a condition of "blessedness or happiness not in the sense of an emotional state but in terms of being in a fortunate situation."[31] The language used in this passage tells us that the blessedness of Christ, which he intends to hand on to those who hear and act according to these norms, will not fade because of outward circumstances, or mere physical or emotional feelings.

Another notable characteristic of the Beatitudes is this: There are no verbs in the original Greek text of Jesus' teaching. For example, a literal translation of the first Beatitude would probably read, "Oh, the blessedness of the poor in spirit."[32] This indicates that the Beatitudes are first and foremost the initiative of God's grace and not the result of our activity. Remember that grace is always first. Our virtuous action is always the right response to grace. Thus, the Beatitudes occupy a unique space as both blessings bestowed freely by God and as requirements for how we should act in our life of discipleship in order to receive those blessings. Again, this was true for the ancient Israelites, and it remains true for disciples throughout Christian history.

I remember the moment when the Beatitudes took up residence in my mind and heart. I was a relatively new Catholic, only two or three years into my journey of discipleship, attending a ministry training conference. I felt the need to receive the Sacrament of Reconciliation, and I wanted to ensure that it would be a great confession, so I knew that I needed a deep and thorough examination of conscience. Instead of looking to the dozens of traditional examinations that I might have found, the Holy Spirit prompted me to turn to the Beatitudes, asking God to show me where these dispositions and actions had been in my life, and where they had been lacking. It was the best examination of conscience ever, and the confession turned out to be one of the best, too! This experience taught me in a profound way that every disciple of Christ must seek to become a person of beatitude. These eight dispositions described by Christ allow us to become holy and truly happy, just as God intends us to be.

Poverty of spirit
"Blessed are the poor in spirit, for theirs is the kingdom of heaven" *(Mt 5:3).*

This first Beatitude stands in stark contrast to the response of the rich young man we discussed near the beginning of this book. He was focused on the kingdom of the world, on all the things that could make him wealthy or powerful, and he was attached to those things.

Ultimately, poverty of spirit is the detachment that happens after a real and transformative encounter with Jesus. Poverty of spirit leads to generous renunciations of possessions like Zacchaeus's, or fishermen walking away from their nets. Detachment from the things and statuses of this world leads to humility, the realization that everything belongs to the Lord and that he is in control.

Poverty of spirit combats its opposites, which are pride, inflated ego, and self-aggrandizement. Father Thomas Dubay, a great spiritual writer of the twentieth century, tells us that "an omnipresent egoism" is the most pervasive trait found among sinners (that's all of us).[33] In other words, we might say that almost every person suffers from a deep and pervasive pride that is not easily overcome. Therefore, we know that Jesus lists this Beatitude first because he knows that it will be the antidote to the capital sin that is rooted most thoroughly in each of us.

In seeking conversion and deeper discipleship, we must ask where we have succumbed to pride. We must ask how we can learn humility and detachment. I have found that the best way is to pray the Litany of Humility every day. God will provide plenty of opportunities to grow in this essential virtue if we're willing to ask him for it.

Mourning

"Blessed are those who mourn, for they shall be comforted" (Mt 5:4).

Saint Augustine, the great Doctor of the Church, teaches us that mourning is "sorrow arising from the loss of things held dear."[34] It can include sadness at the death of a friend or relative, but it also means deep sadness and sorrow at the loss of innocence and holiness. We should be mournful over the state of sin in our own lives and in the world.

Along with such sorrow and sadness comes a willingness to suffer in reparation for sin. From the example Jesus provides during his earthly life and ministry, this is the only acceptable and effective response.

We see blessed mourning in the disposition and actions of the Samaritan woman at the well. Already she has suffered much because of her social situation. After encountering Jesus, when she lays down her water jar and returns to the town, she is ready to embrace more suffering, as she might not be accepted. Although she knows her own sinfulness, she will not continue in it or be held captive by it.

In the life and process of conversion to which Jesus calls us, we must ask for the grace to be strong to face sadness and darkness without succumbing to them. To remain steadfast, we must be willing to pray and suffer. It will not be easy, but it will bring the reward of God's comfort amid suffering.

Meekness
"Blessed are the meek, for they shall inherit the earth" (Mt 5:5).

The first thing we must do is avoid the common misunderstanding that meekness means weakness. Meekness is not weakness! Peter Kreeft, another sage of our time, writes that meekness is "submissiveness to God, not to the world."[35] Meekness is also authority under control, not allowing anger or greed to affect our thoughts and decisions.

In his commentary on the Sermon on the Mount, Augustine teaches us that meekness means overcoming evil with good. He encourages his audience to understand that meekness is the opposite of quarreling and fighting for earthly, temporal goods. Instead, the meek person fights for the higher good.

These two Beatitudes help us to gain control over the passions that arise within us and the difficult situations that arise outside of us. Thus, they are expressions of the virtues of temperance and fortitude.

Hunger and thirst for righteousness
"Blessed are those who hunger and thirst for righteousness, for they shall be satisfied" (Mt 5:6).

Hunger and thirst are two of the most powerful physical feelings that we can experience. Jesus is, no doubt, telling us that there is a spiritual hunger and thirst that will only be satisfied by right relationship with God. The words that are translated from Hebrew (*tsadiyq*) and Greek (*dikaiosunē*) mean to convey conformity to the will of God.

The search for right relationship with God requires conversion, because we are the ones who, by our fallen nature and our sinful actions, are outside of this right relationship. We recognize some of this feeling in our search to make things right in our earthly relationships. Perhaps we have said things like "I would do anything to be in a relationship with that woman," or "I would do anything to have my children back in my life."

The disciples on the road to Emmaus are the biblical example here. They have a deep hope for the salvation of Israel, and they have spent much time following someone they thought would fulfill that hope. Later, they notice that their hearts have burned because of the truth that has been presented to them. Then they rise from dinner, and they undertake a long and dangerous hike in order to tell others about the good news they have just received. They will not let anything get in the way of their new and solid relationship with Jesus.

Mercy
"Blessed are the merciful, for they shall obtain mercy" (Mt 5:7).

This Beatitude is interesting because the reward is the same as the attitude and action that one is living. By living mercifully, we receive greater mercy. This ought to reveal to us that when we live mercifully we are already participating in the very life of God. In fact, we know that mercy is God's greatest attribute.

The Hebrew word that is translated as "mercy" is *chesed* (pronounced hə-said). *Chesed* is "steadfast love, one able to keep alive a relationship forever, regardless of what happens."[36] This is precisely the steadfast love that caused the father of the prodigal son to watch, day after day, for his son's return. This is precisely the love that the woman at the well sought in all the wrong places.

At various points in my life, I have felt very much like the prodigal son and the woman at the well. In those moments, I have felt and known God's *chesed*, his unending mercy, and I have been restored. That restoration, that feeling and knowledge that God loves me beyond my mistakes, allows me to practice mercy more frequently and perfectly with my family or in my job. I can come to imitate the father of the prodigal son instead of remaining as the prodigal son. Better yet, I can become more like Jesus in his dealing with the Samaritan woman at the well, reaching out to build and sustain relationships regardless of what has happened in the past.

This is one of the most difficult Beatitudes to live. It is easier to sow justice, giving to each what we think he or she deserves. Mercy is hard. It is not easy to forgive when we have been wronged, or to forgive criminals who commit the foulest crimes against our family members or our communities. Yet we can look to Jesus' clear teaching (Mt 18:21–22) and his perfect example on the cross: "Father, forgive them; for they know not what they do" (Lk 23:34).

Purity of heart
"Blessed are the pure in heart, for they shall see God" (Mt 5:8).

The word "pure" should stand out to us here. The Greek word is *katharoi*, which is the root of our English terms "catharsis" and "cathartic." When something is cathartic, it has a purifying, cleansing effect. Catharsis is the act of purifying the spirit and emotions. Once the spirit and emotions are purified, a person can focus on one thing and one thing alone.[37]

Beyond the Greek text, the Hebrew concept that is being translated here is extremely important. In Hebrew culture, ritual purity is the only way to enter into proximity and relationship to God. This is why King David writes in Psalm 51, "Create in me a clean heart, O God" (Ps 51:10). David's heart (his mind, his emotions, and his will) had become about one thing: entering into intimate relationship with God. Jesus tells us in this Beatitude that when a person's heart becomes about only one thing, that person will see the face of God.

I see a connection here to the story of Bartimaeus. The blind man's life has become about one thing: seeing rightly. To that end, he calls out to Jesus, "Son of David," and he will not be silenced. His answer to Jesus' question is basically, "I want to see!" His heart has been cleansed in such a way that the first thing, the first person, he sees upon having his sight restored is the God-man himself.

When Bartimaeus exclaims, "Master, let me receive my sight" (Mk 10:51), we can translate that into an even simpler request: "I want a pure heart!" We can only see if we are rid of the things that blind the eyes of our heart.

Peacemaking
"Blessed are the peacemakers, for they shall be called sons of God" (Mt 5:9).

There are two terms that we obviously should unpack for a moment here. The first is "peacemakers." Again, the Greek translation of the Hebrew concept is important here. The Greek authors are trying to convey the Hebrew term, *shalom*, which can mean "safety, harmony, prosperity, health, well-being, or the absence of war."[38] Those who seek to make *shalom* seek to bring about any and all of these qualities in the lives of individuals and communities.

The other term that is ripe for meditation is "sons of God." Throughout the Old Testament, sons of God were people — men and women — who maintained right relationship with the Lord, and Jesus draws that forward as he establishes the kingdom of God. Still, this term takes on a deeper meaning as the Son of God, the Messiah, makes claims of divinity. This Beatitude comes to mean that those who make *shalom* will become divinized in some way. If God is the great giver of peace, then those who make peace in this world will take on God's very life, just as sons take on the life principle, the nature, of their fathers. This is why Athanasius could say, teaching against the Arian heresy, that "the Word was made flesh in order that we might be made gods."

It is also interesting that Jesus, the Son of God, makes peace through his sacrifice. Paul tells us that Christ "[makes] peace by the blood of his cross" (Col 1:20). Peace, then, is made by acts of reconciliation, even sacrificial acts that result in the shedding of blood.

Think also of the parable of the prodigal son, and the father's merciful dealing with his older son. He longs for the safety of his younger son and rejoices at his safe return, but he also seeks harmony between his two sons. He knows that this harmony between his children will create prosperity, health, and well-being within his household, and he is willing to sacrifice himself for that *shalom*. This is the way of the heavenly Father.

Enduring persecution

"Blessed are those who are persecuted for righteousness' sake, for theirs is the kingdom of heaven" (Mt 5:10).

The last Beatitude that Jesus gives us is, perhaps, the most difficult of all. This is why it is the capstone statement. This tells us that the result of right relationship with God is persecution. Why would we want that?

Unlike in the previous seven statements, Jesus adds further explanation to this one: "Blessed are you when men revile you and persecute you and utter all kinds of evil against you falsely on my account. Rejoice and be glad, for your reward is great in heaven, for so men persecuted the prophets who were before you"

(Mt 5:11–12). This blessing statement should remind us that persecution for the sake of right relationship with God is the lot of all
God's holy people. Without fail, throughout salvation and Church
history, those who have sought and lived the life of beatitude have
been persecuted, some in small ways, others to their deaths.

This Beatitude presents the kingdom of heaven as the gift
for living in this way. Recall that the very first Beatitude offers
this same reward. The fact that the first and last Beatitudes tell
us that our reward is the kingdom of heaven shows that all the
other rewards of the Beatitudes are a part of inheriting the kingdom of God. If we are living in the kingdom of God, we will
receive comfort in mourning; we will exercise our gifts, talents,
and authority well; we will live by the rule of mercy; we will
seek only God's perfect will; and we will make *shalom* in human
relationships. It will not be easy, but it will be blessed. As with all
the Beatitudes, we must ask God for the grace of conversion to
embrace this aspect of the blessed life.

All the Beatitudes express essentially one reality. Each of the
qualities of those who are blessed reflects some aspect of right
relationship with God, beginning with a poverty of spirit that
recognizes our place before God. Each of the corresponding
blessings highlights that "all the several kinds of blessedness are
aspects of the one supreme blessing of possessing the Kingdom of
Heaven."[39]

By way of conclusion, it is good to look at the final statement
of blessedness in the life of discipleship (Mt 5:12). After listing all
the blessing statements and their corresponding rewards, Jesus
commands those who would take up this life to "rejoice and be
glad," even in the face of certain persecution. Here, Jesus reminds
us that the result of living beatitude, regardless of the passing
situations of this world, is joy and gladness. Along this lifelong
journey of conversion, we are continually invited into deeper joy
and gladness.

QUESTIONS FOR DEEPER
UNDERSTANDING AND REFLECTION

1. Why do you think that the Beatitudes are the first teachings that Jesus gave?

2. Is there one Beatitude that you understand more completely than the others, perhaps because of an experience in your life? Which Beatitude is it? Why?

3. What is the proper response for Christians who mourn the loss of holiness in the world? Is there something that we can do other than simply talk about the evils we see in the world around us?

4. How are you working in your life to achieve purity of heart, willing one thing only? What are some obstacles you face in living out this Beatitude?

5. When have you experienced the deep peace of knowing that you are a son or daughter of God? Can you describe the experience? What can you do to grow in this realization and live that peace more fully?

Epilogue

LASTING JOY AND PEACE

A ll conversion leads to joy and peace.
     Jesus' every encounter throughout the four Gospels reveals that joy and peace are the lasting effects we will receive by entering into the life of conversion, discipleship, freedom, and mission. The more we turn toward Jesus, the more we are converted, and the deeper and more abiding will be our joy and peace.

The final pages of the Gospel narratives provide quite a few memorable instances of the words "joy," "rejoice," or "rejoicing." At Jerusalem, after the Emmaus encounter, we read that the disciples and apostles "disbelieved for joy" as Jesus stood in their midst (Lk 24:41). Then, in the very last sentence of his Gospel account, Luke tells us about the apostles' response after Jesus' Ascension: "And they worshiped him, and returned to Jerusalem with great joy" (Lk 24:52).

During his teaching at the Last Supper, Jesus tells us that he is the vine and we are the branches; we must abide in him if we are to glorify the heavenly Father, be his disciples, and bear fruit for the kingdom. Then he says, "These things I have spoken to you ... that your joy may be full" (Jn 15:11). Discipleship is ordered toward joy! Moreover, when the Holy Spirit comes, we learn that "sorrow will turn into joy," and when we see Jesus again (after our own bodily resurrection) our hearts will rejoice, and it will not be possible to take our joy from us (Jn 16:20, 22). All we must do, Jesus teaches, is "ask, and you will receive, that your joy may be full" (Jn 16:24).

For one final teaching on joy, we can look to Jesus' high priestly prayer in John 17. Jesus prays to the Father "that they may have *my* joy fulfilled in themselves" (verse 13; emphasis added). This is simply incredible! Jesus has taken on human flesh, lived thirty years of silence and obscurity, engaged in a three-year public ministry, and is about to go to the cross. He has done this all for the sake of his eternal joy, the joy of the Trinity, coming to us and remaining with us. This is the whole point of everything Jesus teaches, and it is the whole point of entering into a life of conversion: to enter into the perfect, abiding, full joy of the Trinity.

Jesus' greatest, final gift

Now we have plenty of evidence that joy is one lasting fruit of conversion. What about the other? Peace. Peace is a tranquility that occurs within our minds, hearts, and lives because things are rightly ordered, and because we as individuals are rightly ordered.

Jesus says something powerful as he promises to send the Holy Spirit upon the apostles and disciples: "Peace I leave with you; my peace I give to you; not as the world gives do I give to you" (Jn 14:27). Jesus, through the mission of the Holy Spirit, intends for us to have the tranquility of right order. This, of course, is not something that the world can offer us, no matter how many parties we attend or how much money we make. It is only from the Lord. It is a precious gift that we should seek, and we should cling to it when he bestows it upon us.

Again, toward the end of his Last Supper discourse, Jesus promises that life in the world will bring tribulation, even scattering of his flock. Still, he concludes by teaching, "I have said this to you, that in me you may have peace. In the world you have tribulation; but be of good cheer, I have overcome the world" (Jn 16:33). The right order that the Lord brings will stand firm against anything that the enemy and the world might heap up to try to knock us down. When we know that, we can always be peaceful, because we know that the Lord is fighting for us and he has already won the victory.

The last point about peace that I want to draw out comes from John 20. On the day of the Resurrection, when the doors of the Upper Room are locked, Jesus stands among his apostles and says to them, twice, "Peace be with you" (19–21). He does not say, "See, guys, I told you that I would come out of the grave after you saw me hanging on that Roman torture tree." He does not say, "Now we can get on with our work." The first word he speaks to them is "Peace." Peace is the first gift Jesus bestows after the Resurrection. And because we are living in the age of the Resurrection, we have access to peace perpetually. Peace is always with us!

Immediately following his statement, Jesus breathes on the apostles and bestows the Holy Spirit upon them. This should tell us that the lasting peace that is possible, the lasting peace we seek, happens because we are imbued with the Spirit, because we live under his guidance and direction. It is only God, in the person of the Holy Spirit, who gifts us with right order in our lives and lasting tranquility.

The biblical characters we have met in this study all came to a deeper joy and to "the peace of God, which passes all understanding" (Phil 4:4–7) through their encounters with Christ. In meeting Jesus, they have been led home from a far country. They have been led beyond simply living according to commandments and rules to true repentance, to trust and cruciformity, to freedom, and to discipleship and mission. When we enter into our own journey of ongoing, daily conversion, we will travel the same trajectory and receive these same gifts. By reading, studying, and praying these stories from the Gospels, we will receive the grace we need to continue that journey of conversion, day after day, and enter into the blessedness Christ promises.

BIBLIOGRAPHY

Adams, James Rowe. *From Literal to Literary: The Essential Reference Book for Biblical Metaphors*. Cleveland, OH: The Pilgrim Press, 2005.

Aquinas, Thomas. *Summa Theologiae*. Kindle.

Augustine. *On the Sermon on the Mount*. www.newadvent.org/fathers/1601.htm.

———. *Tractates on the Gospel of John*. www.newadvent.org/fathers/1701.htm.

Barron, Robert. *The Priority of Christ: Toward a Post-Liberal Catholicism*. Grand Rapids, MI: Brazos Press, 2007.

Bauer, Walter. *A Greek-English Lexicon of the New Testament and Other Early Christian Literature*, 3rd ed. Revised and edited by Frederick W. Danker. Chicago: University of Chicago Press, 2000.

Bernard of Clairvaux. "On Conversion." In *Bernard of Clairvaux: Selected Works*. Mahwa, NJ: Paulist Press, 1987.

Brown, Colin, ed. *The New International Dictionary of New Testament Theology*. Vol. 2. Grand Rapids, MI: Zondervan, 1979.

Catholic Commentary on Sacred Scripture. 16 vols. Grand Rapids, MI: Baker Academic, 2008–2018.

Dubay, Thomas. *Deep Conversion, Deep Prayer.* San Francisco: Ignatius Press, 2006.

Hahn, Scott, and Curtis Mitch. *The Gospel According to John.* Ignatius Catholic Study Bible. San Francisco: Ignatius Press, 2003.

———— *The Gospel According to Luke.* Ignatius Catholic Study Bible. San Francisco: Ignatius Press, 2001.

———— *The Gospel According to Mark.* Ignatius Catholic Study Bible. San Francisco: Ignatius Press, 2001.

John Paul II. Reflection on Ad limina visit. May 31, 1988.

————. *Veritatis Splendor* ("The Splendor of Truth"). August 6, 1993.

Kierkegaard, Sören. *Purity of Heart Is to Will One Thing.* New York: HarperOne, 2008.

Kreeft, Peter. *Back to Virtue.* San Francisco: Ignatius Press, 1992.

The Navarre Bible: New Testament. New York: Scepter Publishers, 2008.

Oden, Thomas C., ed. *Ancient Christian Commentary on Scripture.* 29 vols. Downers Grove, IL: InterVarsity Press, 2003.

Weddell, Sherry A. *Forming Intentional Disciples: The Path to Knowing and Following Jesus.* Huntington, IN: Our Sunday Visitor, 2012.

NOTES

1. Granted, selling literally everything we own may be something the Lord asks of some of us as we draw nearer to him. But that is outside the scope of this book, and never recommended without plenty of advance prayer, discernment, and advice from a trusted spiritual guide.

2. Walter Bauer, *A Greek-English Lexicon of the New Testament and Other Early Christian Literature*, 3rd ed., revised and edited by Frederick W. Danker (Chicago: University of Chicago Press, 2000), sub voce "ὑπάρχω," 1029.

3. Ibid., s.v. "κτῆμα," 572; and F. Selter, "Possessions," in *The New International Dictionary of New Testament Theology*, vol. 2, edited by Colin Brown (Grand Rapids, MI: Zondervan, 1979), 846–847. In Matthew's version of this Gospel passage, there are two different Greek words that are translated as "possessions." We have dealt with one of them, the one that Jesus spoke. The other is *ktemata*, which refers specifically to the material goods that a person owns. Matthew uses this word at the end of the passage, "When the young man heard this he went away sorrowful; for he had great possessions [*ktemata*]" (Mt 19:22). Matthew employs these two different Greek words to make it clear that the young man didn't understand exactly what Jesus was saying in this moment.

4. There is an excellent, although short, treatment of this theme by Scott Hahn and Curtis Mitch in *The Gospel of Luke.* Ignatius Catholic Study Bible, 2nd ed. (San Francisco: Ignatius Press, 2011), 51.

5. Robert Barron, *The Priority of Christ* (Grand Rapids, MI: Brazos Press, 2007), 76–85; and commentary on John 4:1–45 in *The Navarre Bible,* (New York: Scepter Publishers, 2008), 376.

6. Bauer, *A Greek-English Lexicon*, s.v. "βίος," 176–177.

7. Bernard of Clairvaux, "On Conversion," in *Bernard of Clairvaux: Selected Works* (Mahwah, NJ: Paulist Press, 1987), 68.

8. Quoted in *Ancient Christian Commentary on Scripture*, ed. Thomas C. Oden, New Testament vol. 3, Luke, ed. Arthur Just Jr. (Downers Grove, IL: InterVarsity Press, 2003), 382.

9. Timothy Johnson, *The Gospel of Luke* (Collegeville, MN: The Liturgical Press, 1991), 88.

10. Joel Green, *The Gospel of Luke* (Grand Rapids, MI: Eerdmans, 1997), 235.

11. Hahn and Mitch, *The Gospel of John*, 24.

12. Son of Isaac, one of the patriarchs in Genesis. Jacob's name was changed to Israel.

13. Augustine, *Tractates on the Gospel of John*, 15.10.

14. Barron, *The Priority of Christ*, 89.

15. Ibid.

16. The Revised Standard Version of the Bible doesn't capture this connection nearly as well as other translations, including the New American Bible. Still, the ancient, original languages are abundantly clear. Jesus states that he is the same God who reveals himself to Moses in the Sinai desert.

17. Augustine, *Tractates on the Gospel of John*, 15.30.

18. The other commandment that Jesus gave during his public ministry is "Do this in remembrance of me," when he instituted the Eucharist (see Lk 22:19).

19. I must admit that my deep appreciation and understanding of this scriptural episode began by listening to a presentation by then-Father Robert Barron, entitled "Following the Call of Christ: Biblical Stories of Conversion." It has been more than ten years since I heard that presentation. Some of the ideas in this chapter may come directly from Barron, while others are completely my own, emanating from years of study and reflection. I am deeply appreciative of Bishop Barron for his

scholarship, his presentation, and the work that his organization does for evangelization and conversion.

20. Quoted in Thomas C. Oden and Christopher A. Hall, eds., *Ancient Christian Commentary on Sacred Scripture, New Testament*, vol. 2 (Downers Grove, IL: InterVarsity Press, 1998), 152.

21. Mary Healy, *The Gospel of Mark* (Grand Rapids, MI: Baker Academic, 2008), 217.

22. Ibid.

23. Thomas Aquinas, *Summa Theologiae* 2.2.30.4

24. Healy, *The Gospel of Mark*, 217.

25. "The Way" is the most common name given to the religion of the disciples of Jesus in the Acts of the Apostles. The most prominent passages include Acts 9:2, in which Saul of Tarsus is preparing to persecute the followers of Jesus; Acts 19:9, when Paul is engaged in apologetics with people in Ephesus; and Acts 24, while Paul is on trial before Felix, the Roman governor of Caesarea.

26. Quoted in Just, *Luke*, 290.

27. Ibid., 291.

28. William Barclay, *The Gospel of Luke*, rev. ed. The Daily Study Bible Series (Louisville, KY: Westminster John Knox Press, 1975), 235.

29. Quoted in Just, *Luke*, 290.

30. This is borne out in the other places in the Gospel where the same word is used to describe Jesus' audience (e.g., Mt 9:35–38; 14:13–21; Mt 15:29–31; Lk 5:1–3; 7:24–35).

31. Curtis Mitch and Edward Sri, *The Gospel of Matthew*, Catholic Commentary on Sacred Scripture (Grand Rapids, MI: Baker Academic, 2010), 87.

32. William Barclay, *The Gospel of Matthew*, The Daily Study Bible Series rev. ed., vol. 1 (Philadelphia: The Westminster Press, 1975), 88.

33. Thomas Dubay, *Deep Conversion, Deep Prayer* (San Francisco: Ignatius Press, 2006), loc. 171, Kindle.

34. Augustine, *On the Sermon on the Mount*, 1.2.5, http://www.newadvent.org/fathers/16011.htm.

35. Peter Kreeft, *Back to Virtue* (San Francisco: Ignatius Press, 1992), 141.

36. "Mercy," Taizé, May 7, 2008, https://www.taize.fr /en_article6825.html.

37. For an in-depth philosophical treatment of this concept, see Sören Kierkegaard, *Purity of Heart Is to Will One Thing*, recently republished by several publishers.

38. James Rowe Adams, *From Literal to Literary: The Essential Reference Book for Biblical Metaphors* (Cleveland, OH: The Pilgrim Press, 2005), 212.

39. C. H. Dodd, *More New Testament Studies* (Grand Rapids, MI: Eerdmans, 1968), 7, quoted in Mitch and Sri, *The Gospel of Matthew*, 88. See also W. D. Davies and Dale C. Allison, *A Critical and Exegetical Commentary on The Gospel According to Matthew*, vol. 1 (London: T&T Clark, 1988), 446, for commentary on this statement's presence in the first Beatitude.

ACKNOWLEDGMENTS

I would like to thank my wife, for having the patience and diligence to care for our family while I was writing this book. I would also like to thank Father David Graham, my pastor and boss, for affording me a flexible work schedule while I wrote. Perhaps most importantly, I would like to thank Father Bill Parham, who gave me my start in parish ministry and the lion's share of my understanding of Scripture and theology. Father Bill read an early manuscript of this book and offered suggestions to hone my thought and expression about Jewish culture along with Greek and Latin words and concepts. Jon Jones, a friend and fellow scholar, also aided with finding sources. Finally, I would like to acknowledge the faculty at the Augustine Institute in Denver, my alma mater, for helping me become a theologian and giving me the understanding of the centrality of conversion in the Christian life.

ABOUT THE AUTHOR

DEREK ROTTY is husband to Khira and father to five wonderful, beautiful, energetic, hungry children. He was born into a Christian family and home, and he came into full communion with the Catholic Church at the Easter Vigil in 2004. He began serving as a lay parish minister in 2005. Since then, he has worked at multiple parishes across the country, serving children, teens, adults, and families. In ministry, his primary mission is to help people encounter the love and grace of God, which will transform their lives. In his spare time, he enjoys great books, good food, inexpensive wine, and baseball.